LIBERTY, EQUALITY & DEMOCRACY

LIBERTY, EQUALITY & DEMOCRACY

By Chris Berg

CONNOR COURT PUBLISHING

INSTITUTE OF PUBLIC AFFAIRS

Connor Court Publishing Pty Ltd
Institute of Public Affairs
Copyright © Chris Berg 2015

Connor Court Publishing

PO Box 224W

Ballarat VIC 3350

sales@connorcourt.com

www.connorcourt.com

Institute of Public Affairs

Level 2

410 Collins St

Melbourne VIC 3000

ipa@ipa.org.au

www.ipa.org.au

ISBN: 9781925138566 (pbk.)

For Bronwyn, Leonard and Walter.

Chris Berg is a Senior Fellow with the Institute of Public Affairs and a prominent columnist and political commentator. He is the author of *In Defence of Freedom of Speech: from Ancient Greece to Andrew Bolt* (2012) and *The Growth of Australia's Regulatory State: Ideology, Accountability, and the Mega-regulators* (2008).

I would like to particularly thank Richard Allsop, Mikayla Novak, and John Roskam for their feedback and comments.

Contents

FOREWORD

By Tim Wilson
Australia's Human Rights Commissioner

Everywhere you look democracy is being tested. For the second time in a century it appears to be delivering significantly perverse results in Europe. Local polling identifies the public is complacent about the very system of government that protects the freedom for Australians to express their view.

But these are only the superficial threats. This is a wonderfully timely, sobering and mischievous book. It penetrates the camouflaged, pervasive threats to democracy, but rarely draws fire.

Berg's analysis is both intuitive and refreshing. His recognition of the rule by experts is particularly prescient. Democracy is about a distrust and recognition of the shortcomings of centralised authority. Yet we are increasingly told to trust expert opinion and follow their judgement.

Government is particularly good at propagating this culture through the supply of jobs and funding for so-called 'experts' through the academy, appointed 'expert panels', state-sponsored 'think tanks', and, dare I say, Commissioners.

Berg refers to the preference for decisions by 'experts' as an 'independence fetish'. He's partly right. Their existence is an expression of democratic will. Their attraction is a simple detailed answer to a defined problem. But their beautiful solutions are often dependent on the 'independence' that comes from not needing to weigh recommendations against competing public policy objectives and the appetite of the public.

The model can be particularly dangerous if democratic processes appease their interest to have power independent of a political framework.

Experts have their place. They shouldn't have the final say. That should sit with the people.

Berg's analysis of the anti-democratic undertones of paternalism is particularly relevant. Paternalistic 'nudges' and 'shoves' are increasingly presented as caring elitist virtue. In practice it is the fullest expression of contemptuous vice from those whose arguments don't carry public sympathy. For them democracy is a frustration, and a hindrance.

Human rights and democracy are intrinsically linked. Human rights rest on the radical idea that every individual should have equal opportunity to be free to pursue their lives and their enterprise and be treated equally by law.

Democracy is the ultimate expression of formal equality. Under democracy everyone is equal before government and the law. Further, everyone is equal to have their say about how both evolve and operate. The trade-off from that bargain is that they are equally susceptible to the consequences of their decisions.

Democracy is a compact. The beauty of the marketplace is that it relies on voluntary cooperation and exchange. By its nature the state does not. As Berg argues democracy 'does not grant rulers any superhuman or superior qualities … The existing political order is only maintained through negotiation and bargaining'. It is democracy that forces voluntary cooperation into the considerations of the state.

Berg concludes 'democracy is terrifying' because 'nobody has the "right" to rule'. It rebuffs the human instinct for security and predictability. Good, and may that ever be so. Democracy shifts political power to the hands of the many, not the few.

March 2015

INTRODUCTION

THE ARGUMENT

When Thomas Rainsborough stood up in a church in South London late October 1647, he gave us one of the most perfect expressions of the democratic ethic: 'For really I think that the poorest he that is in England hath a life to live, as the greatest he.'[1]

This book is about that idea. The idea that all people have the same fundamental moral worth. The idea that all lives are equal. The idea all people's interests deserve to be weighted equivalently. It is a deeply intuitive idea. It is the core idea at the heart of democracy. But as this book will argue, it is also an incredibly radical idea, which in many ways flies in the face of many of our most fundamental political and economic beliefs.

To be 'democratic' is much more than accepting people have the right to vote. It is to accept that everybody has a right not to be ruled—that everybody has a sphere in which they can and must make their own choices about their own lives. Put it this way: if we don't believe our fellow citizens are intellectually capable of deciding what and how much to eat, whether to drink, or how to arrange their financial affairs, then why do we think they are capable of voting? Democracy is not just a system of changing political leaders. It is a ethical claim about the relationship between state and citizen, and about individual equality.

Ideas do not come out of nowhere. They are grounded in specific historical events and conceived by real, fallible people. Thomas Rainsborough was one of the radical participants at the Putney Debates, when the army of the English parliament, in open rebellion against the Stuart monarchy, argued out the shape of the England they were fighting to build.

The preceding months in 1647 had seen the army march into London. The most senior army officers—Oliver Cromwell among them—were trying to negotiate a settlement with Charles I. Yet the army was divided among itself as to the political settlement that should replace the old order. Senior officers favoured parliamentary reform and the expansion of the franchise, yet also wanted to maintain the monarchy. A group of lower-ranked radicals favoured far more revolutionary policies—universal male suffrage, freedom of religion, equality under the law, and parliamentary sovereignty.

The radicals in that extraordinary meeting have come to be known as Levellers. Like so many political movements, the Levellers were named by their enemies. The Levellers, wrote one royalist opponent, was a most apt title for such a despicable and desperate knot to be known by, that endeavour to cast down and level the enclosures of nobility, gentry and property, to make us all even, so that every Jack shall vie with a gentleman and every gentleman be made a Jack.[2]

The political vision offered by the Levellers at the Putney debates is strikingly modern. They imagined a free England characterised by freedom of speech, religious toleration, equality before the law, open and free markets, civil rights and an end to the abuses of the Star Chamber. Nearly four centuries later we can recognise these demands as the central tenet of liberalism—an assertion of individual rights against the power of the state.

The Levellers were democrats, too. They wanted a written constitution. And they demanded the right to vote—universal manhood suffrage, not limited by property or class. The document they circulated before the debates, simply titled 'An Agreement with the People' insisted that every person be subject to the same law, 'bound alike', and 'no tenure, estate, charter, degree, birth or place do confer any exemption from the ordinary course of legal proceedings whereunto others are subjected.'[3]

When the Agreement was read aloud on the second day of the Putney debates, Henry Ireton, Cromwell's son-in-law, honed in on the document's first clause, one which outlined the principles by which parliamentary representation should be recalculated:

That the people of England, being at this day very unequally distributed by counties, cities, and boroughs, for the election of their deputies in Parliament, ought to be more indifferently proportioned, according to the number of the inhabitants; the circumstances whereof, for number, place, and manner, are to be set down before the end of this present Parliament.[4]

Ireton was unsure what this meant. Was this a call to redraw the franchise according to ancient principles of the English constitution before the Norman Conquest? If so, he would have no objection. But, Ireton argued, if,

> It is said, they are to be distributed according to the number of the inhabitants: 'The people of England,' etc. And this doth make me think that the meaning is, that every man that is an inhabitant is to be equally considered, and to have an equal voice in the election of those representers, the persons that are for the general Representative; and if that be the meaning, then I have something to say against it.[5]

This was the great sticking point for the more conservative senior officers. Was the civil war fought to reestablish ancient lost rights, or was it to establish new ones? It was reasonable to believe, in their mind, that the perfidy and corruption of the Stuart kings had undermined a great English tradition of liberty. But the 'fundamental constitution' of England gave the franchise only to those who owned land and trading corporations; it was they 'who, taken together, do comprehend the local interest of the kingdom'. English birth came with rights, but the responsibility for forming the political community rested with those who had a landed or commercial stake in the kingdom.

Thomas Rainsborough, a colonial and the highest ranking member of the Levellers, did not demure. Ireton's fears were correct. The Levellers wanted not just a restored ancient franchise but universal male suffrage. 'Every man born in England', Rainsborough argued 'cannot, ought not, neither by the Law of God nor the Law of Nature, to be exempted from the choice of those who are to make laws for him to live under, and for him, for aught I know, to lose his life under.' He went on:

> every man that is to live under a government ought first by his own consent to put himself under that government; and I do think that the poorest man in England is not at all bound in a strict sense to that government that he hath not had a voice to put himself under.[6]

Almost every twenty-first century reader would believe that they are fully in accord with Rainsborough's views. Almost everybody would say they believe human beings are equal—or ought to be treated as equal. Our democratic system is supposed to reflect this truism. We, as citizens, all have the right to participate in that system, to vote for our elected representatives who act as our agents in the operation of government.

But in fact we live in a world fundamentally at odds with the Levellers' ideals. Despite our protestations of the importance of democracy, we live in a fundamentally anti-democratic age.

This book is an exploration of the basic moral core of democracy and its implications. Each individual is, from the perspective of the political and legal system, fundamentally equal. Each individual has the same moral worth as the other. All have the same rights, deserve the same protections, and should be treated equivalently under the law. Human moral equality is a deeply intuitive belief—it is the ethical basis that motivates much of our claims about what is 'fair' or 'just'. A situation is unfair when an individual is treated differently from another on the basis of their background, their ethnicity, or their wealth. Justice has been denied when the law does not give each party to a dispute equal weight. Democracy is a political system designed to reflect that essential moral equality of all individuals.

And yet it is widely acknowledged that we are living through a crisis of democracy. Survey after survey shows the dissatisfaction with government is at a distressing low. In 2012 the Australian think tank the Lowy Institute for International Policy published a poll with a striking finding: 40 per cent of Australians do not agree with the statement that 'democracy is preferable to any other kind of government'. Breaking the population down by age, the poll was even more worrying. Of the 18-29 year old cohort, nearly 60 per cent disagree that democracy is most preferable.[7]

This Lowy poll was no outlier. It has been repeated, with remarkable consistency, each year since. A 2014 edition of the Lowy poll fleshed out some of the nuances. Of the 40 per cent of Australians unimpressed by democracy, 21 per cent agreed that 'a more authoritarian system where leaders can make decisions without the processes of democracy achieves better results'. However, many more appear to be disappointed with the way democracy has manifested in the twenty-first century, rather than the idea of democracy itself. Thirty-six per cent agreed 'I have become disillusioned with Australian politics and think another system might work better', 42 per cent agreed with the statement 'democracy only serves the interests of a few and not the majority of society'—an ironic reversion on the old belief that democracy would dangerously empower the masses—and 45 per cent believed that 'democracy is not working because there is no real difference between the policies of the major parties'.[8]

Other polls confirm Lowy's findings. The Australian Constitutional Values survey, published by Griffith University in 2014, found that just 52 per cent of Australians had good or very good confidence that the federal government would do a good job carrying out its responsibilities. Voters are similarly pessimistic about state and local governments.[9] Reporting this poll, the media focused on what it believed was a precipitous decline in faith in the federal government in recent years. (The first Australian Constitutional Values survey, in 2008, found that 81 per cent of Australians had good trust and confidence in the federal government.) A newspaper report on the findings declared that '[d]ysfunctional government has created a crisis of faith in our political leadership'.[10] Yet other levels of governments have similarly poor reputations.

Another survey, the Australian National University's governance and democracy poll, has consistently found a much higher relative satisfaction with democracy than the Lowy poll. In the 2014 ANU poll, 72 per cent of respondents reported that they are very or fairly satisfied with the way democracy works in Australia. Yet this seemingly high figure is the lowest it has been in seven years. And in other ways the ANU poll is consistent with other measures. Just 43 per cent of people believe that it makes a difference which party wins the election. Only 56 per cent of people believe that their vote counts. The ANU poll also asks how much confidence respondents had in various social and political institutions. The most trusted institution in 2014 was the Australian Defence Force, in which 40 per cent said that had a 'great deal' of confidence. The least trusted institutions were unions and federal parliament, with a bare six per cent each.[11]

This dissatisfaction with the shape of Australian politics and political institutions was dramatically manifest in the 2013 federal election. In September 2013 nearly a quarter of Australians—23.5 per cent of those who cast a vote—chose to vote against *all* the major parties as their first preference in the Senate. These voters rejected Labor, the Liberal Party, the Nationals, and the Greens alike.[12] The 2013 anti-major vote was around double the comparable figure in the three federal elections previously, which were 13 per cent in 2010, 11 per cent in 2007, and 12 per cent in 2004.

The much higher than normal non-major vote had practical consequences. Six of the 12 new Senators to enter parliament after the 2013 election were from non-major parties—Family First, the Liberal Democrats, Palmer United, and the Motoring Enthusiasts Party. While most commentary about this remarkable result focused on either the complexities of preferential voting or the ambiguous motivations of the mining billionaire Clive Palmer, such a final tally would not have been possible if there hadn't been such a high non-major vote in the first place.

In September 2014 the ABC's *Lateline* program compiled a series of reports on what it saw as democratic disenchantment. Academics, activists and former politicians lined up to offer their indictment of the state of Australian democracy. 'Both the political parties have been more interested in coming to power, rather than serving the people', said one academic. Another proclaimed that Australian politics is 'boring, it's dishonest and it doesn't actually get us anywhere at all because everybody spends most of their time trying to beat each other up rather than give us good ideas'. Ged Kearney, the president of the Australian Council of Trade Unions complained about 'short-term jingoistic politics from politicians who are obsessed with the next media release'. She also said 'I think we need to find new ways for people to feel that they can influence political outcomes. Clearly an election is not that.'[13]

Yet, as the political historian Murray Goot has pointed out, claims that Australians are excessively cynical and unhappy with their democracy date back almost to federation.[14] Apathy and scepticism may just be a traditional theme of Australian political culture. One study of letter writers during the Great Depression found widespread complaints about the greed, dishonesty and self-interest of the political class.[15] The 1930s was of course an era where dissatisfaction of democracy manifested itself in support for much less benign political movements than that espoused by the Palmer United Party. Goot assembles evidence to suggest that, in fact, Australians' engagement with politics remains remarkably stable over a period of decades. On some measures—for instance, interest in political campaigns—there has been rather substantial improvement. And while fewer Australians now rate politicians as having high or very high ethics or honesty as they did since the 1970s, that drop in prestige is been nothing compared to the decline in prestige of other professions, such as bank managers and lawyers.

Nevertheless, even if it has a long history or has been exaggerated, democratic dissatisfaction still presents a serious puzzle, and a serious problem. Democratic legitimacy is founded on the consent of the governed. We have a problem if the governed have lost faith in the entire project.

So what explains the disenchantment, disengagement and the unhappiness with the political system? There has been a wealth of explanations advanced. It is, for instance, tempting to blame poor leadership. Australia has certainly had a succession of uninspiring political leaders. A Melbourne University poll in 2013 found that 57 per cent of people agreed that the 'tone of political debate in Australia' was 'noticeably worse' than it had been in the past.[16] Fifty-eight per cent believed that political leadership was also worse than in the past. But it is easy to be nostalgic about leadership. As Lord Bryce wrote all the way back in 1921,

> Every traveller who, curious in political affairs, enquires in the countries which he visits how their legislative bodies are working, receives from the elder men the same discouraging answer. They tell him, in terms much the same everywhere, that there is less brilliant speaking than in the days of their own youth, that the tone of manners has declined, that the best citizens are less disposed to enter the Chamber, that its proceedings are less fully reported and excite less interest, that a seat in it confers less social status, and that, for one reason or another, the respect felt for it has waned.[17]

Another popular explanation is that the democratic virtues have been replaced by commercial ones. One typical example of this argument is provided by Tim Soutphommasane, now Australia's Race Discrimination Commissioner. Soutphommansane wrote in response to the 2012 Lowy Poll that 'we are losing our very ability to talk about a common good … The logic of buying and selling, of self-enrichment, increasingly governs our social and civic life.' We have almost completely transitioned 'from market economy to market society'. In his view, the desire for personal wealth now dominates popular consciousness. As a consequence, '[s]ome of us seem to be asking: why have democracy if something else could deliver greater personal wealth?'[18]

Soutphommasane is half right. He is correct to identify that democracy is not simply an instrument by which we vote to nominate political representatives. It is a more substantial and more consequential philosophy; an expression of deep seated social values. He is also correct when he suggests that public support for democracy has waned as the values which underpin it have been undermined.

Yet there's a powerful irony in Soutphommasane's argument. Blaming the decline of democracy on citizens for pursuing their own values—and we have been told repeatedly that 'consumerism' and 'materialism' are philosophical values—is, this book shall argue, exactly the sort of disdain for the masses that has created the democratic crisis in the first place.

Recent decades have seen a sustained intellectual assault against the idea of human rationality. Psychologists and behavioural economists have built a large body of evidence about our inherent and deep failures in reasoning and cognition. Particularly in the realm of public health, activists and bureaucrats have used that evidence to call for massive legal intervention in the personal decisions of citizens—products ought to be banned, limited and controlled on the basis that consumers are unable to make the best decisions for themselves.

So, to put the question we posed at the beginning of the book more gently, if we believe that consumer society places so many barriers to decision making—through advertising, deception, and the high cost of acquiring information to be clever consumers—that those decisions drop below some minimum threshold for rationality, why do we not believe the same thing about decisions made in the political arena? The people who shop and the people who vote are the same people. Yet we praise individual choice in the political sphere while condemning it in the commercial sphere.

The Levellers understood the fundamental ethic value underpinning democracy: the basic moral equality of all individuals. It's easy to brush over how radical this idea is. For almost all of its history humans have lived in social orders constructed around hierarchies. Those hierarchies were based on religions, divine rights, racial categories, nationalistic and ethnic divisions, or simply the brute strength of power that maintained monarchs and autocrats in their privileged states. Democracy rejects those hierarchies. It claims that all people have the right to participation. All people are both capable of choosing the political framework that they live under, and any attempt to supplant that right is unjust and invalid—anti-democratic. As we shall show, this reasoning has some significant and largely unrecognised consequences.

By necessity, this book ranges over a vast amount of history and political concepts. The philosophy and practice of democracy is an incredibly broad topic, even without considering how it relates to liberty and equality. It is necessary right at the outset to spell out the overall argument.

Chapter 1 outlines the basic argument of the book—the notion of political equality as the philosophical foundation of a democratic order. It finds its origins in the idea that the state is a contract between free individuals to make collective decisions. Democracy is much more than the outward manifestations of elections and legislatures. It describes the relationship not between citizen and state but between citizen and citizen: it is a philosophy of cooperation, rather than an instrument of political control. Discussion about democracy often confuses the mechanisms of a democratic system with its philosophical underpinnings. Yet even the twentieth century's worst dictatorships have given themselves democratic frills. What those dictatorships lack is the foundational ethic of democracy: the idea of the state as a contract between free and equal citizens, and the rejection of natural hierarchy and authority that this idea implies.

While the first chapter looks at democracy as an ideal, the three subsequent chapters look at democracy as it exists.

Chapter 2 offers a survey of the development of the voting franchise. The chapter focuses on the United Kingdom, as it is that country in which modern liberal democracy first sprouted. All governments, whether autocratic or democratic, have to be formed by some sort of coalition. No ruler is absolute. A ruler needs the support of a group of influential people to stay in power. Dictators live under the constant threat of being overthrown by their subordinates. So in a very real way, that group of supporters are the 'franchise'. The question is how—and why—that franchise expanded to become universal suffrage. The answer is not too dissimilar from the ideal model of the democratic contract espoused in chapter 1. The franchise evolved as a 'bargain' between rulers and ruled, with one of the main triggers for changes in the bargain being changes in taxation. The phrase 'no taxation without representation' only dates from the eighteenth century but its sentiment dates back to the medieval era, and has driven political change up to the present day.

Chapter 3 continues the descriptive analysis by looking at democracy as it operates today. No defence of democracy ought to be based on a naïve faith in democracy as a system of government. Democratic decision-making is sub-optimal in many ways. Voters suffer deep cognitive biases that make it hard for them to make the best political choices. They harbour systemically wrong views about public policy, and have little incentive to become more informed. Elections are imperfect mechanisms for controlling politicians. The complexity of modern government makes it impossible for voters or elected representatives to fully understand the levers of power they nonetheless wield. This litany of failure creates a problem for those who would defend democracy on an instrumental basis—it just isn't very good at producing ideal policy and translating the preferences of voters into government action.

Chapter 4 looks at one popular answer to the problems raised in chapter 3—the idea of rule by experts. If voters and politicians are as incapable as the evidence suggests they are, then surely handing over policy decision making power to experts might give us better government? This was the core idea behind Plato's philosopher-kings, who, by virtue of their great intellect, could rule for the benefit of the people. Their legitimacy came from their superior governance. Expert rule appeals most to those who feel that their preferred policies have not been sufficiently supported by the electorate. But expert rule is based on a fundamentally flawed premise. Even before we consider the legitimacy of a government based on a hierarchy of intelligence, the much-vaunted experts are as susceptible to exactly the same sort of cognitive biases and systemic errors as the general population. And experts are especially vulnerable to overconfidence; a flaw in reasoning which can have dangerous consequences for public policy. In chapter 4 we also discuss one challenge to the cult of political expertise—the Athenian model of 'sortition', the allocation of public office by random chance. That sortition is such an intellectual challenge to the modern mindset demonstrates how deeply we have embedded the idea of expertise as the ultimate governing philosophy, even while professing the virtues of democracy and equality.

Indeed, as chapter 5 shows, the cult of expertise has been chipping away at the structure of democratic government for some time. Governments have been creating government agencies which are formally separated from both democratic lines of accountability and immune to the direction of elected politicians. The idea behind such institutions is to remove 'politics' from policy and decision-making, and let the only driving force behind government action be the expertise of the decision-makers. The most prominent and iconic of these institutions are central banks, but the principle has spread to become a defining one in modern bureaucratic construction. Governments laud the 'independence' of new regulators and advisory boards—apparently finding a great virtue in creating bodies with the powers of a state but without the constraints of democratic legitimisation. The chapter looks at both the philosophical and practical justification for these bodies. Do independent regulators function more effectively than traditional bureaucracies? The evidence isn't as unambiguous as its supporters claim. And without that grounding in practical success, the case for undemocratic rule by experts is threadbare.

Expert guardianship is not the only hierarchical challenge to the doctrine of moral equality. Chapter 6 looks at a particularly pernicious one: racial hierarchy, a division and ordering of human worth according to 'innate' racial characteristics. Such racialist thinking has been used to give one group power over another group with the intellectual justification that either the former group deserves such power or the latter group is unable to wield self-autonomy. The foundation of racialist hierarchy in inequality is explored through the debate between the nineteenth century writer Thomas Carlyle and John Stuart Mill. In response to Carlyle's defence of African slavery as a natural form of hierarchy, Mill presented a value system that has come to be described as 'analytical egalitarianism'. This idea was at the foundation of his utilitarian philosophy. It presupposed that each individual's preferences and desires were morally equivalent: no person could have their preferences overridden just because the preferences of others were superior. The implied ethical basis of the famous phrase 'the greatest happiness for the greatest number' is that each individual within that aggregated set is indistinguishable from the point of view of policy design.

Chapter 7 looks at a less malicious manifestation of hierarchical and anti-democratic sentiment, but a more common one: the disdain for the mass culture and the interests and obsessions of the lower orders that casts itself as a critique of materialism and consumerism. There is a deep intellectual connection between the anti-consumerist thought of the twenty and twenty-first centuries and the anti-democratic thought of centuries earlier. Both worry that the masses, left to their own devices, will be indulgent and pleasure-seeking. Both blame these desires on innate human frailty and the destructive influence of demagogues and marketers respectively. Both argue that the masses harm themselves when they pursue these desires. And both use those arguments as a proposal to override and regulate those desires. This line of thinking has deep cultural and political roots. It forms, for instance, the basis of the censorship of obscenity. But the most visible and politically powerful manifestation of this today is in the field of public health, as paternalistic regulators and activists seek to control the choices of what people consume. The paternalistic worldview is not just a critique of marketplace rationality but of democracy itself.

Chapter 8 looks at the limits of democracy. Do the ethical foundations of democratic government imply that democracy should be unbounded? One possible objection to the claims in Chapter 7 is that paternalistic policies, regardless of their moral bases, are legitimised by the usual principles of representative government. If something has been voted on by elected representatives then how can it be described as undemocratic? This most extreme illustration of this problem was the Nazi seizure of power. In the final elections of the Weimar republic, two-thirds of voters supported parties opposed to the continuation of democracy. The Reichstag vote that gave Adolf Hitler absolute power was not a free vote—Communist Reichstag and a few social democrat members had been excluded—but even had their votes been registered, there was enough support for Hitler's power grab that the measure would have passed anyway. Clearly there is something undemocratic about a vote to abolish a democracy but determining exactly why is harder than it first appears. The argument made in this book also provides principles by which democratic instruments can be limited. The chapter argues that democracy's philosophical underpinnings provide a guide to constraining democratic excess.

This book is a work of synthesis rather than invention. It aims to take a large number of separate strands and phenomena—such as voter dissatisfaction, independent regulatory agencies, paternalism—to weave them into a larger story about constructing a political community and economics system which takes equality seriously.

One assumption we are going to make here is that there is such thing as a state and that it is desirable to have one. In other words, our argument for democratic philosophy is not going to rest on a comparison with a stateless society. Let us assume that governments have to exist in order to provide certain public goods—security, both domestic and foreign, and the enforcement of contracts. In order to provide those goods they have to finance themselves, usually through taxation. Of course, some readers may prefer a state with greater ambitions: the provision of welfare, economic and environmental regulation, funding for the arts, the creation of public parks, community centres, and stadiums. Either way, big or small, these governments have to be formed and legitimised in some way.

Nevertheless, some of the consequences of arguments in this book suggest that, all else being equal, we ought to favour a smaller government rather than a bigger one. The larger the government the more likely that it will violate the moral principles on which democracy is founded. Government is the systemic organisation of coercive power. It is a powerful attraction for those who would like to impose their values on the population, or to elevate certain interests relative to other interests. The larger and more complex a government, the more opportunities there are for these systemically unequal divisions of power to arise.

There is a deep and close relationship between the classical liberal belief in a small government focused on protecting persons and property, and democracy. Yet this relationship has often been challenged. In his study of the Levellers, the Marxist political theorist C. B. Macpherson argued that their support for democracy was strictly limited. In Macpherson's view, the Levellers wanted the franchise to be denied to all those who were either 'servants or beggars', which (depending on whose population figures we use) could mean that barely a third of the English male population would have the vote.[19] If we accept Macpherson's argument, then what seems like high-minded claims of principle were in fact extremely limited. Either the Levellers were being dishonest by professing their support for human equality, or, worse, they did not view servants and beggars as equivalently human.

The evidence for Macpherson's argument is weak. It relies on two statements made by a non-army participant in the

Putney debates. Yet the only record we have of the debates gives no indication that this non-army participant spoke for the Levellers. Indeed, he was directly contradicted by acknowledged Leveller spokesmen like Thomas Rainsborough.[20] When Cromwell asked where the radicals proposed to restrict the franchise, another Leveller, John Wildman, replied:

> Every person in England hath as clear a right to elect his representative as the greatest person in England ... because all government is in the free consent of the people.[21]

Leveller's position was not ambiguous to its opponents. Cromwell and his supporters at the debates were convinced that the Levellers supported manhood suffrage. Cromwell's son-in-law, the general Henry Ireton, professes both confusion and hostility to what he understands to be the Levellers' argument: 'that every man that is an inhabitant is to be equally considered, and to have an equal voice in the election of the representors'. This was hard for Ireton to understand, but it is an accurate paraphrase of the Levellers' views.

How the Levellers understood democratic equality is not academic. Between Macpherson's interpretation and those who have refuted it lies one of the great contests of political theory. The Levellers were individualists. They aggressively and passionately supported the right to life, liberty, and property. They believed in economic rights as much as they believed in civil rights. They argued for individual property ownership and free trade; anticipating many of Adam Smith's great arguments by more than a century. In other words, the Levellers were recognisably classical liberal, to a striking and remarkable degree. When they attacked privilege they attacked the privilege of aristocracy. When they attacked wealth they attacked the wealth of chartered monopolies.[22] As the historian David Wootton writes, 'not only do their objectives have a contemporary ring, but the very language they use is often indistinguishable from our own.'[23]

All history is written with an eye on the present. In the view of mid-twentieth century socialists, to be classically liberal was to ignore or even support entrenched social hierarchy—the hierarchy created by birth or wealth. The unequal distribution of wealth and the unequal distribution of political enfranchisement go hand in hand. Their argument can be phrased another way. Liberals of the early modern era claimed that governments were formed to protect life and property of their citizens. So why would they support giving the property-less classes a vote?

Macpherson was fundamentally wrong. He was wrong on the history. There is no evidence to suggest that the Levellers believed in a limited franchise. But most of all, he was wrong on the philosophy. Using his misunderstanding of the views on democracy expressed at Putney, Macpherson purported to demonstrate that the doctrine of 'possessive individualism'—that is, a classical liberal individualism protecting property rights alongside civil liberties—was opposed to political equality. In other words, that what liberals called 'freedom' was only freedom for some. Free trade liberals were opposed to democratic equality.

To make this argument one would have to wilfully ignore the sentiments expressed by Rainsborough and Wildman. Rainsborough's claim in particular has gone on to be the defining statement of the Putney Debates: 'that the poorest he that is in England hath a life to live, as the greatest he'.

We must be careful not to go too far here. The Levellers spoke of the poorest *he*, not the poorest *she*. Women's suffrage was a step too far for the Levellers—they sought universal manhood suffrage, not universal suffrage. In this they were not at all unusual. Many of the most passionate preachers of the early modern period against the political divisions of privilege appear to have accepted the political divisions of gender, even when that acceptance is inconsistent when measured against their own philosophies.[24] Hierarchy based on gender is a long stain on the development of liberal democracy—even some of the most passionate democrats of the past had this unforgivable blind spot.

Likewise, it is absolutely true that there is a strand of free market thought that is sceptical of democracy. Some are concerned that democracy is not sustainable. In 2012 the Republican presidential candidate Mitt Romney told a private fundraising event that 47 per cent of the American population would vote for the Democratic candidate Barack Obama 'no matter what'—that cohort pays no income tax and are net beneficiaries of the transfer system. The fear is that who gain from redistributive policies will vote for them to be expanded, soaking a smaller and smaller class of taxpayers for more restribution. The ultimate result of that logic is economic collapse, as an economy cannot infinitely sustain more people paying out of the tax system than paying into it. This argument is effectively a variation on old fear of the tyranny of the majority, which will be discussed below.

A more aggressive critique of democracy doubts the moral virtue of the form of government itself. According to this argument, democracy is at best an unfortunate necessity—a tool for smoothing over the transfer of power—but a necessity which threatens to destroy more fundamental values, like individual rights or the free economy. Voters do not always support the most efficient policies. They do not always respect the rights of others. This argument has some obvious truths. But at its most extreme it manifests itself to outright hostility to democracy.

The economist Hans Hermann Hoppe, in his book *Democracy: the God that Failed*, writes that

> [d]emocracy promotes shortsightedness, capital waste, irresponsibility, and moral relativism. It leads to permanent compulsory income and wealth redistribution and legal uncertainty. It is counterproductive. It promotes demagoguery and egalitarianism.[25]

In Hoppe's view, democracy is a system of communal ownership—a variant of communism—and a more liberty and property-rights respecting political system is monarchy, where the monarch 'owns' the public goods and acts as a caretaker in the same way property owners look after their property. Hoppe's claims need not detain us, except only as a curiosity. But he represents a radical outlier of a strand of anti-democratic thinking which is common on all sides of the political spectrum—the anti-democratic thought which fears the 'anarchism' that results when all people are consulted.

Democracy is not well-loved. Thinkers from left, right, and 'the sensible-centre' have accidentally collaborated in a mutual project to undermine its most central precepts. As this book will argue, democracy's moral underpinning—the principle of human equality—is a more radical doctrine than is commonly understood, and is under attack from angles that few have recognised. We must recognise the flaws of government, the limits of politics, the problems of democratic instruments, yet, at the same time, recognise the deeper, more fundamental truth that democracy reflects: all people have exactly the same right to participate in the construction of a political community.

CHAPTER

ONE

A CONTRACT AMONG EQUALS

It is a peculiar feature of modern dictatorships that they pretend they are democratic. North Korea is one of the most complete totalitarian states the world has ever seen. It is subject to the heredity rule of a military dictatorship. Yet it formally describes itself as the Democratic People's Republic of Korea. Its 2009 constitution affirms that it is run according to the principle of 'democratic centralism'. North Korea is not alone. The preamble of the 1977 Constitution of the Union of Soviet Socialist Republics claimed that the Soviet Union:

> is a society of true democracy, the political system of which ensures effective management of all public affairs, ever more active participation of the working people in run-

ning the state, and the combining of citizen's real rights and freedoms with their obligations and responsibility to society.

This reads absurdly in retrospect. But the Soviet insistence that they were a true democracy was slightly more than just a rhetorical frill. Indeed, the Soviet Union held an enormous number of elections. There were votes on the USSR parliament, national parliaments, and local councils (the eponymous 'Soviets'). One estimate suggested voters were exposed to election campaigns for one eighth of their entire life.[1] The campaigns were extensive and elaborate. Public meetings were staged in workplaces and social events. There would be dozens of articles in the local press. As an election day drew near, electoral officials were trucked in to oversee the smooth operation of the process. And, with an elaborate secret ballot, the Soviet voter would affirm his or her support of the single, Communist Party-approved, official candidate. The victor would then trumpet their 99 per cent turnout and 99 per cent voter support, complete with congratulatory news editorials.[2]

These elections were held not for the benefit of foreign observers. They formed a key part of Soviet ideology—they were rituals that were supposed to affirm that the Soviet hierarchy ruled with the consent of the governed. We should be careful about dismissing this attempt at attaining democratic consent for dictatorship too quickly. It was only half an illusion. The psychology of totalitarianism is complex. As one contemporary Soviet-watcher argued, Soviet elections were analogous to singing a national anthem or saluting a flag. The elections legitimised the regime, even if they were, obvious to outside observers, entirely fraudulent.[3] In the view of Soviet ideologists, the single candidate election reflected a deeper 'truth' about socialism. An editorial in the official Communist Party journal in 1957 proudly argued that the fact voters were not presented with a choice:

> does not mean that such an order of elections is less democratic ... Such a position is fully natural; it expresses the socialist essence of our society, its solidarity, the unity of party and people.[4]

Indeed, there was much in the Soviet electoral system that was superficially democratic. Ballots were secret—an innovation which can be traced back to the Australian secret ballot. They were not marked or numbered. Elections would be preceded by a prolonged and apparently engaging campaign. There was high turnout at the ballot box. And even the fact that voters could only choose a single candidate, as ludicrous as it seems, is not uncommon in the free West. In the United States there are dozens of uncontested House of Representatives seats every election. Australia has seen more than three hundred state and Commonwealth elections where candidates ran unopposed.[5] So what makes the Soviet single-candidate elections more democratic than single-candidate elections in the Australia or the United States?

When most people think of democracy they think of its constituent parts: the formal institutions of voting and governing. In Australia, we have a Commonwealth parliament, split into two houses, and an executive government drawn from that parliament. Australians with citizenship are compelled, by law, to register a vote to elect representatives to that parliament. Democracy, in this sense, is compulsory voting. It is the Australian Electoral Commission. It is political campaigns and stump speeches and election scrutineers and tally rooms.

And so, when we debate 'democracy' we debate it in these

institutional terms. Should voting be compulsory or should citizens be free not to vote? How should votes be counted? Should the winner of an election be decided according to a first-past-the-post system, or some sort of preferential scheme? Single- or multi-member electorates? How—and when—should voters be registered? Then there is the matter of political parties. How should they be funded—through private donations or with taxpayers' money?

These are all important questions. But they tend to confuse the form of a democracy for its substance. When we suggest that one institutional setting is more 'democratic' than another—that preferential voting is more democratic than first past the post, for instance—we pretend that the meaning of democracy is uncontroversial; that there is an agreed mechanism by which we can measure *democratic-ness*. Of course, there is no such thing. Popular conceptions of what constitutes a true 'democracy' are a mass of confusion. The academic conception of democracy is just as fraught: categories and distinctions and definitions piled upon each other that either radically diverge from existing democratic practice, or end up muddled and uncertain.

In a 'direct democracy', all policy decisions are made collectively. Ancient Athens had the classic direct democracy. As we shall discuss in later chapters, in Athenian democracy public offices existed filled by lottery, and policy made by ballot. From the perspective of the twenty-first century, the Athenian system inverts many of the key features of our more familiar 'representative democracy'. In most modern democracies, citizens elect representatives to make legislative decisions for them, and public offices are either elected directly, filled by those who have been elected, or filled by delegates of the elected representatives.

These are not the only distinctions which are commonly made between democratic types. Many people distinguish between 'liberal democracy' and 'social democracy'—a distinction which pivots on the structure of a country's economic and welfare system. Liberal democracies tend towards free markets and often have an Anglosphere heritage. Social democracies have more government intervention and social security, and were found first on the European continent. Other distinctions focus on dominant characteristics of policy making or political engagement. Some scholars write about 'deliberative democracy', in which elected representatives gather legitimacy not merely from their election, but from engaging the population in the decisions themselves. Another typology—'grassroots democracy'—valorises bottom-up community organisation, and seeks to empower activists. In his book *The Life and Death of Democracy*, John Keane conceives of 'monitory' democracy, whose essential characteristic is civil society and non-profit organisations scrutinising the actions of the government and the powerful.[6]

Yet these distinctions join the conversation half way through. They allow us to imagine what an ideal democratic form might look like, but not the terms by which we could judge it. They encourage us to treat democracy as a means to an end—for instance, good government, free markets, socialism, or political engagement—rather than a good in and of itself.

In Putney in 1647 the Levellers did not offer proposals for an electoral system, or debate theoretical ideal democratic types. The case for universal suffrage was not taken for granted in the seventeenth century. The case for equality was not obvious. Throughout Western history, a political order founded on hierarchy has been the rule rather than the exception.[7] It was not immediately obvious to the Levellers' contemporaries and political opponents that democracy ought to be pursued. There were serious arguments for political systems based on principles of hierarchy.

So instead, the Levellers articulated the principles upon which governments ought to be democratic in the first place. If we take those principles as our starting point—rather than focusing on the outward manifestations of democratic practice— then it becomes clear that democracy is a much more profound and important philosophy than commonly understood.

Writing four decades after the Putney debates, John Locke faced a very different political environment to the Levellers. The Stuart monarchy had been restored. The radicalism of the Civil War was a vivid memory. But Locke's masterpiece, *Two Treatises of Government*, published in 1689, is a fundamentally radical work.[8] Locke took the uncompromising liberalism of the Levellers and built a political and economic philosophy around their call for liberty. Locke's argument for liberty, property rights, and government by consent is ultimately founded on his principle of equality: 'all Men by Nature are equal'.

This was not an assertion of naïve egalitarianism. There were many social circumstances where the equality was not the sole concern. One could gain a 'just Precedency' in society through unique virtue, or age, or merit. To recognise natural equality was not to deny individual excellence. The division of labour is, indeed, based on this: that some people better at performing some tasks than others—in Locke's words 'the different degrees of industry' that men display—and that individuals ought to specialise where they can add the most value. Furthermore, Locke did not claim that natural equality did not mean that there could not be, justly, inequality of wealth. His political philosophy supported the right to private property, even when that right led to a 'disproportionate and unequal' pattern of wealth distribution. For Locke, a society ought to value excellence and merit, but

> all this consists with the equality, which all men are in, in respect of jurisdiction or dominion one over another ... being that equal right, that every man hath, to his natural freedom, without being subjected to the will or authority of any other man.[9]

In other words, while society may divide according to ability or virtue, the overriding presumption must be that humans have an inherent or innate natural equality, underpinning the political society in which they form.

From that equality, Locke derived a social contract theory of government. As Locke saw the social contract, individuals form political communities—and form governments—because they desire to protect their lives and their property. In modern language, governments are formed to supply the public goods of security and a just legal system. Locke was no anarchist. That government would harness coercive power: the cost of that security and law would have to be borne by the free inhabitants of the political community, and would therefore require taxation, a bureaucracy, and an executive government.

The social contract was not Locke's invention. It can be traced back to ancient philosophy and early religious texts: Genesis records God making a form of social contract with the natural world when he declares an 'everlasting covenant between God and every living creature of all flesh that is upon the earth'.[10] But history had demonstrated to Locke as it has demonstrated to us that governments, once constituted, can become tyrannical. In the words of Saint Augustine in his *City of God,* 'remove justice, and what are kingdoms but gangs of criminals on a large scale?'

So for Locke, governments are only legitimate for as long as they have the consent of the governed. That consent depends on how successfully they protect lives and property. If a government becomes malignant—if it neglects its responsibilities to protect life and property, or impinges the liberties of the citizens—those citizens have a right to dissolve that government. The social contract has been broken.

Of course, there never was an original social contract. A century after Locke wrote his *Two Treatises,* David Hume and Adam Smith ridiculed the notion that government originally formed as the result of freely contracting individuals.[11] Smith, in his *Lectures on Jurisprudence,* raised the most obvious objections. Actually existing governments did not form in such a collegial manner. There is no evidence to suggest, nor any reason to believe, that our ancestors gave their consent for governments to appropriate the fruits of their labour or hold a monopoly on violence. Nor, even if such evidence could be attained, would there be any reason to believe that a contract willing entered by our forebears would be binding on us. Finally, and most critically, simple observation offered no support for the original contract ideal:

> Ask a day porter or day-labourer why he obeys the civil magistrate, he will tell you that it is right to do so, that he sees others do it, that he would be punished if he refused to do it, or perhaps that it is a sin against God not to do it. But you will never hear him mention a contract as the foundation of his obedience.[12]

A more radical critique of the social contract is offered by feminist and race scholars. Carole Pateman in her book 1988 book *Sexual Contract* and Charles W. Mills in his 1997 book *The Racial Contract* argued influentially that the liberal social contract theory was an exclusionary one.[13] For both these writers, the social contract was actually a contract between representatives of a white male class to facilitate the subjugation of women and non-whites respectively. Mills writes that 'the Racial Contract is an exploitation contract that creates global European economic domination and national white racial privilege.'[14] For Pateman, 'men's freedom and women's subjection are created through the original contract—and the character of civil freedom cannot be understood without the missing half of the story that reveals how men's patriarchal right over women is established through contract'.[15] In their view, liberal theorists have, at best, missed an elementary hierarchical relationship underpinning the so-called egalitarian contract, or, at worst, deliberately engineered that contract to be a dominating one. In other words, the universalism of the social contract and its notions of human equality are fictitious.

If the racial contract and the sexual contract are meant solely to be descriptive accounts of the development of the world then there is little that could be doubted about them. Hierarchies based on race and gender have been endemic in human history, and the charge that they have been systemically and self-interestedly ignored is absolutely correct. The great natural rights theorists of the American revolution did not extend those rights to the slaves that many of them owned. Likewise, it is a rare early modern liberal who granted to women the same rights as men. Locke, most damningly, made the claim that women in marriage ought to be subordinate to men; a gaping hole in his doctrine of political equality.

So is the social contract a fiction to be discarded? No. One

of the twentieth century's most incisive social contract theorists, James M. Buchanan, put it this way: 'The relevance of the
contract theory must lie ... not in its explanation of the origin
of government, but in its potential aid in perfecting existing
institutions of government.'[16] It cannot be denied that the history of government is the history of coercion, slavery, empire,
conquest, and oppression. The notion of a social contract is
not a claim about history. Locke did not believe, in a literal
sense, that no person could have their natural freedom taken
away without their consent: the experience of the Tudor authoritarianism, Stuart authoritarianism, and Cromwellian authoritarianism would have taught him that. No, for Locke and
Buchanan a just political order was one founded on a current
social contract. The status quo may be have been born in blood-
shed or revolution or tyranny. In that sense, the social contract
is a myth. But the task before us is to create the political order
we do desire, defend the desirable elements of what exists and
discard the undesirable.

The social contract is an analytical construct to understand
and idealise what values a free democratic state should reflect.
In the modern era, we are more used to thinking of constitutions as simply detailing the procedures of legislation and
executive government; how bills are made, how the executive
is funded, and the process whereby parliament is resolved.
Australia's constitution is archetypally utilitarian in this sense.
After a brief preamble declaring that the states have united to
form a Federal Commonwealth, the text gets to the business
of business of defining the nation's sovereignty and building a
parliament.

But in the early modern era, when the very idea of democratic government was novel and untested, the creation of a

constitution was as much an act of political philosophy as it was institutional rule-making. Early social contract thinking drew its idea of a political contract from a religious covenant. In fifteenth and sixteenth century Europe, believers formed separatist communities in which their worship could, hopefully, be free and their doctrines respected. These communities obviously had to be entirely voluntary. They could not prevent members from leaving. And as they were not states in any sense they had to develop codes which bound the community by agreement, and which described the community's relationship to God. In many striking ways these covenants resemble the constitutions of today. Describing how such a Godly community was constituted and gathered, one English clergyman wrote in 1616 in striking terms:

> By a free mutuall consent of Believers joyning and covenanting to live as members of a holy Society together in all religious and vertuous duties as Christ and his Apostles did institute and practise in the Gospell. By such free mutuall consent also all Civill perfect Corporations did first beginne.[17]

No surprise then that the religious dissenters which made up the Leveller movement saw their ideal commonwealth in a similar way. The Agreement of the People was, as its title indicated, an agreement—a proposed contract between free and equal citizens. As one edition of the agreement stated:

> Having by our late labours and hazards made it appear to the world at how high a rate we value our just freedom, and God having so far owned our cause as to deliver the enemies thereof into our hands, we do now hold ourselves bound in mutual duty to each other to take the best care we can for the future to avoid both the danger of returning into a slavish condition and the chargeable remedy of another war.[18]

It is worth pointing out that the form these constitutional documents take is a contract between individuals who are, in the formation of that community, on the same political rank. They offer no hierarchy, save that between God and humanity. They are not a negotiation with monarchs or the aristocracy. They are an assertion of political community before political leadership. So, too, was the Constitution of the United States, which famously begins:

> We the People of the United States, in Order to form a more perfect Union, establish Justice, insure domestic Tranquility, provide for the common defence, promote the general Welfare, and secure the Blessings of Liberty to ourselves and our Posterity, do ordain and establish this Constitution for the United States of America.

It is worth dwelling upon just how radical this conceit was. Most of the great liberal documents of the past were not agreements between equal citizens but concessions by the ruler towards the rights of the citizen. In 1215 the Magna Carta established a compact between King John and the English barons. The preamble opens with a greeting from 'John, by the grace of God, king of England, lord of Ireland, duke of Normandy and Aquitaine, and count of Anjou' to his subjects. Then came a series of justifications for the great charter. First, that such a charter would honour God. Second, that it would improve the King's soul. Third, that it would honour the church. Finally, it would improve the realm.[19] (The fifth and most important reason for the Magna Carta was unstated: the rebel barons leading the 'army of God' safely ensconced within the City of London.) Yes, John was under duress. But that did not stop the Magna Carta from being framed as if it was being handed down to the people from the king above.

The early modern revolutionaries jettisoned that pretence. Rather than specifying the relationship between the ruler and the ruled, they sought to specify the relationship between free citizens. In their view that relationship existed before—and was superior to—the government. They understood that democracy was not merely a set of rules, or a collection of institutions, or a series of elections. It was a compact between equal citizens to form a political community. This ought to be the first and superior governing principle of a modern democracy.

This chapter opened with an exploration of the strangely democratic trappings of totalitarian states. Like the Soviet Union, even the North Korean hermit kingdom—a nation with the population size of Australia controlled absolutely by the Kims for more than half a century—feels the need to dress itself up as an electoral democracy, with universal suffrage and the secret ballot. Of course, as a totalitarian regime, the ballot is not, in practice secret, and the number of political prisoners puts a lie to claims of universal suffrage.

Yet we should not dismiss these democratic frills as merely the remnants of a long forgotten democratic Marxist ideology. (All mention of communism was stripped from the North Korean constitution in 2009.) The monarchs of the early modern world did not feel any need to pretend they had been placed there by the people: they had been placed in their role by God, or tradition, or the natural hierarchical order.

By contrast, the totalitarians of the twentieth and twenty-first century believe that a democratic veneer (no matter how transparently deceitful) is a necessary safeguard of their power. All governments feel they have to at least pretend to have popular legitimacy, that the citizen and the state

are bound together in a reciprocal, contract-type relationship—and that political authority derives from some sort of
participation in communal decision making. Even the most
totalitarian.

CHAPTER

TWO

A BARGAIN WITH TAXPAYERS

Every political system—whether it is democratic, autocratic, theocratic, monarchical, or republican—has electors. Every political system has to be founded on the basis of some sort of coalition; there has to be a group of people who protect the leader and sustain their power. The idea of a one-person rule is a fiction: even a ruler that styles themselves a god king needs supporters. God kings are as liable to being deposed as any other rulers. Their professed divinity cannot protect them from regicide.

As the political scientists Bruce Bueno de Mesquita and Alastair Smith argue, the difference between an elected democratic leader and an autocratic ruler is one of degree rather than kind, at least insofar as each require the support of a coalition to sustain their power.[1] In every political system there are a number of 'influentials' who determine who the ruler is going to be. In a democracy those influentials are drawn from a very large pool of voters. Yet they ultimately represent a narrow sample of that pool: say, for instance, swinging voters in marginal seats. It is those swinging voters who determine who the ruler will be, rather than the total pool of voters. In a dictatorship both the pool and the influentials are much smaller—for instance, the upper echelons of the military, business or the party bureaucracy. The regular purges that are so characteristic of dictatorial regimes demonstrate violently how important it is for dictators to ensure their coalitions are strong and their power is protected.

The need for rulers to have the support of a coalition in even monarchical or authoritarian systems helps explain why parliaments existed long before democracy did. It is possible to trace, however discontinuously, the origins of the English parliamentary system all the way back to the Roman era—to the Germanic assemblies described by the Roman historian Tacitus at the end of the first century AD.[2] This chapter tells that story—how the governing councils of ancient tribes evolved into the rich parliamentary institutions of today. We emphasise here why those evolutions occurred, in an effort to rehabilitate the descriptive content of social contract theory. The extension of the franchise from the Germanic assembly all the way to universal suffrage in the early twentieth century was driven in the most part by the need to strike a bargain between taxpayers and rulers.

The Germanic assembly was known as the *thing*, a name which lives on in the parliament of many Nordic nations (The Danish, Norwegian, and Icelandic parliaments are called the

Folketing, Storting, and Alþingi respectively.) As Tacitus describes the assemblies, they constituted a group of armed men, headed by a king or chieftain. The leaders would put up proposals, to which the assembly would either yell their dissent or clash their arms in approval. This was, from what we understand from Tacitus, a primarily military council, in keeping with the militaristic nature of the Germanic tribes. The kings themselves were elected by the assemblies. We can imagine the Germanic tribes as sort of a cooperative venture whose goal was conquest. The assemblies established trust between entrepreneurial chieftains and their warriors.[3]

The migration of the Germanic Angles, Saxons and Jutes after the end of the Roman occupation brought Germanic traditions to Britain. The assemblies evolved into something that we now call the witenagemot, an assembly of the ruling class to advise the king that existed between the seventh and eleventh centuries. This body, often today called the witan (which more accurately describes its members), assumed legendary status in early modern Britain as the parliament of the 'ancient constitution' that protected British liberties until it was crushed under the Norman yoke in 1066. In fact, the witenagemot was more like a king's council than a modern parliament. It was comprised solely of a small group of nobles, princes, judges, clergymen and administrators, numbering perhaps as low as a dozen to as high as one hundred. The king chose who was to join the assembly. The king summoned the meetings, chose the venue, determined the agenda, and decided when the meetings were to be dismissed. Yet the witenagemot also had much autonomy. The witenagemot acted both as legislature and chief judiciary; approving the king's bills and hearing criminal and civil cases that related to the aristocracy or the monarch. As

Henry Maine wrote, 'In the infancy of society many conceptions are found blended together which are now distinct, and many associations which are now inseparable from particular processes or institutions are not found coupled with them.'[4] The most important function of the witenagemot was exercised rarely. It elected the king.

There is no reason to believe that the witenagemot ever acted in opposition to the wishes of the king, or believed itself to be a separate governing body—it was an extension of the king's power, rather than an oppositional political force. All social institutions exist as the result of a bargaining process. The witenagemot was a mechanism for distributing the gains of power between the king's supporting coalition. Another purpose of the king's council was information gathering.[5] One of the challenges facing an autocrat is the vast amount of information needed to rule the realm—no king can gather enough data to rule effectively by themselves. Thus a king's council, comprised only of the most reliable and loyal members of the kingdom, was a way to delegate information gathering.

Whatever its purpose, the democratic 'franchise' was limited to members of the witenagemot. Democratic equality, such as it was, was limited to only those members of the council, and they were subservient to the king. The development of democratisation over the subsequent millennia consists in the struggle against both these limitations—the expansion of the franchise all the way to universal suffrage, and the attainment of parliamentary supremacy over the king.

It was a decision of the witenagemot that led to the Norman invasion. When, upon the death of Edward the Confessor in 1066, the witenagemot decided that his brother-in-law, Harold, the Duke of Wessex would be the new king.

This decision sparked two separate invasions by rivals to the crown. The first was by Harald Hardrada of Norway, with the support of Harold's brother Tostig. Harold repelled this invasion in a battle outside York. The second was by William, Duke of Normandy, who believed that Edward had nominated him as heir a few years before his death and that therefore the decision of the witenagemot was illegitimate. William invaded England through the south, defeating the English defenders, killing Harold in the process, and laying claim to England for the Normans.

The Norman conquest of England reduced, but did not eliminate, the influence and importance of the witenagemot. The witenagemot was slowly replaced by a system of councils. Felix Liebermann writes that 'Almost every single feature was radically changed; nevertheless the continuity between the witana gemot and [William the Conqueror's] Great council is a tenet to be decidedly upheld.'[6] Over the centuries the legislative and judicial functions of the king's council were separated. A 'Permanent' or 'Continual' Council of the chief advisors to the king evolved into the Privy Council. A 'Great Council', consisting of all nobility and noble clergy of the realm, was brought together by writ and assembled only for special purposes.

The word 'parliament' first entered the British lexicon in the early thirteenth century. What made parliaments different from the assorted councils of earlier medieval origin was that they included the commons—nominated representatives from the boroughs. We discuss the commons below. Like the councils, parliament was first and foremost an information gathering exercise. It was easier for the king to summon representatives than to personally tour his realm.[7] One historian writes that 'parliament was not a 'self-perpetuating corporation' dedicated to advancing the cause of liberty, but rather part of the machinery of government.'[8]

Yet parliament grew to have another function: gathering assent for crown appropriations. Kings were expected to live off the income from their crown lands and customary charges. But in the middle and late medieval period these revenues were in decline. The practice of granting lower lease rates to the king's favoured nobles—that is, delivering benefits to the ruling coalition—undermined the monarchy's revenue base. Furthermore, the demands of constant warfare placed increasing pressure on the expenditure side of the king's budget. To expropriate more revenues the crown had to tax the barons. But this undermined the authority of the king among the barons, who understandably resented being taxed for decisions in which they had no authority. A. V. Dicey wrote that 'It was only a weak or tyrannical King—a John or a Richard II—who neglected to ask counsel; for the ruler who acted without the advice of his great men distinctly outrage the moral feeling of his day.'[9] Parliament was the venue for this counsel.

The principle that new taxes required some sort of consent dated back to the Magna Carta in 1215—that foundational document of liberty which told the monarchy that they ruled in partnership with the aristocracy. King John had levied no less than ten special levies for his attempt to hold and then reclaim Normandy. When the barons rebelled, they extracted concessions from John that established the principle that taxation could only be imposed 'by the common council of our kingdom'. Among the establishment of some basic civil liberties, it was this requirement that had the most long term effect on the development of English democracy. The Magna Carta was hardly constitutionally rigid—the document had to be constantly reaffirmed over the following centuries—but the idea that parliament had a jurisdiction over revenue raising gave that body oversight over almost every function of government.

One fascinating denouement of the episode occurred just a few years after the Magna Carta was signed. A council of barons was assembled under Henry III and approval was given to raise a new tax. However, the Bishop of Winchester had been absent from that council, and when he was approached to produce the requisite 159 marks, he objected. The exchequer upheld his objection on the grounds that he had not personally consented to the collection of the tax and was not therefore liable to pay it. As one historian reflected, this incident

> shows how far the statesmen of the day were from realizing the principles of modern political theory. They had not yet grasped the conception of a Council endowed with constitutional authority to impose its will on a dissenting minority. Here it was apparently a minority of one.[10]

When, in subsequent decades, the principle was established that a majority decision overrode the minority, it was a significant victory for the monarch. Bruce Bueno de Mesquita and Alastair Smith talk about how important it is for rulers seeking stability to narrow the number of influential voters to a smaller subset than total eligible voters. The rule that all voters are bound by the decisions of the majority achieved that goal. (In later chapters we will discuss another historical episode where the consent required more than a simple majority—the *Sejm* of the Polish-Lithuanian Commonwealth.)

But why include the non-nobility? The House of Commons has its origins in the decision to include four knights from each county and two representatives from each major town in parliaments convened by the rebellious Simon de Montfort in 1264 and 1265. Edward I's writ for the parliament of 1295 proclaimed that 'what touches all, should be approved of all, and it is also clear that common dangers should be met by measures agreed upon in common', and the principle was fixed that representatives from the cities and boroughs should attend each parliament. In the short term, the significance of the commons was that it effectively brought the nascent English commercial sector into the political bargain.[11]

In the fifteenth century the rules by which representatives of the commons were chosen became formalised. Those rules remained relatively stable for the better part of four centuries. The voting franchise for the members was based on ownership of land worth at least 40 shillings. Representatives had to live in their communities and were subject to the same property requirements. The size of the boroughs was not determined by population. These rules enfranchised around five per cent of the male population. That figure grew over time. Between the establishment of parliament and the early industrial revolution, inflation and economic growth very slowly increased the number of people who met the franchise qualification from five per cent to around ten per cent of the total male population.[12] In other ways, however, the franchise became less 'representative'. The uneven distribution of population between boroughs created the so-called 'rotten boroughs' in the eighteenth and nineteenth centuries, where some traditional boroughs had very low numbers of enfranchised voters, allowing small groups or families to control seats for centuries.

It was a rare parliament that was convened without seeking a grant. For instance, Henry VII, who reigned between 1485 and 1509, summoned seven parliaments, only one of which did not end with a request for finances.[13] Throughout the medieval period parliament only had a casting vote on questions relating to taxation. While kings consulted parliament on other matters, they only felt bound on tax decisions. Nevertheless parliamentary approval of the king's wishes offered legitimacy and, of course, kept parliament on side for when tax matters were to be decided. The bargain between king and parliament changed over time, gradually granting parliament domain over policy questions not directly related to tax. Control of the purse strings of government deepened parliamentary control over the business of government. Given the incredible cost of wars, parliaments began to involve themselves in foreign policy questions.

Parliament carved out further responsibilities when kings tried to exceed their traditional bounds. Henry VIII sought to legitimise his expropriation of the Catholic Church by seeking parliamentary approval. Closing the monasteries and confiscating their assets gave Henry a large amount of wealth which he used to wage war and buy support. Much of the church's wealth was in land. Appropriating that land would increase Henry's financial self-sufficiency, which he hoped would reduce parliament's authority. Yet his decision to seek parliamentary approval for the confiscation just further empowered parliament, giving the body authority over questions of religion. And it established the principle that the decisions of the legislature were supreme—superior to royal will or divine revelation.[14]

The principle of parliamentary supremacy was made concrete by the tumultuous seventeenth century. The events leading up to the English Civil War permanently damaged royal authority in a number of ways. Charles I sought revenue for war against Spain and France that parliament was not willing to give. He therefore sought to exploit traditional sources of revenue to raise funds. But his aggressive exploitation of traditional and ancient taxes—such as import taxes on wine and forced loans—was seen as arbitrary and tyrannical. And they did not prevent him from being forced to eventually call parliament to request further income.

When Charles finally called a parliament in 1640 (it had been more than ten years since the last parliament was acrimoniously dissolved), the legislature was in a strong bargaining position. It extracted both a reaffirmation of the medieval parliamentary authority that the Charles and his predecessor James I had undermined, but also a requirement that parliament sit both regularly (at least once every three years) and a rule which prevented the monarch from unilaterally dissolving the parliament. Yet these concessions, significant as they were, did nothing to temper the constitutional crisis. Parliament was emboldened and began to press for further authority. But this power grab split the legislature into a parliamentary and royalist factions, a train of events which eventually led to outright civil war, Charles I's execution, and the establishment of the Commonwealth.

What made the civil war truly 'revolutionary' was however separate to this long running power contest between parliament and monarch. The civil war brought about fervent ideological, philosophical and religious innovation. The Levellers, the early political liberals discussed in the introduction, were just one of many groups and ideologies which flourished among the political chaos. The other major political radicals were also the Diggers, a recognisably proto-socialist group named after their communal farming practices. (In his book *The World Turned Upside Down*, the Marxist historian Christopher Hill regrets that it was the Levellers, rather than the Diggers, whose ideas emerged from this period ascendant.[15])

There was also kaleidoscope of religious innovators. Some of those survived the seventeenth century to become established religious orders—the Baptists and the Quakers, for instance. Others, like the Fifth Monarchists, the Seekers, the Ranters, and the Muggletonians, did not. Nevertheless, what unified all these disparate and often religiously or politically opposed groups was the sense that the established order—whether economic, religious, or constitutional—had collapsed. The hierarchies of the post-Norman conquest were being abandoned and a new world could take its place. When the old order was forcefully restored by the return of Charles II in 1660, many dissenters left to the newly established American colonies to pursue their vision.

With Restoration, the slow constitutional contest between monarch and parliament resumed, but the ideological consequences of the civil war were long lived. From that time on, any claims to parliamentary authority were made in the shadow of the more radical claims advanced about suffrage and natural rights during the civil war. The Glorious Revolution of 1688 presented parliament another opportunity to establish autonomy against the king. The English Civil War had resulted in one-man rule. English constitutional reform would now be iterative—minor changes leading up to long term change. Indeed, the Bill of Rights, passed in 1689 to define the clarify the relationship between monarch and legislature, differed very little from the existing settlement. What was being established by the constant repetition of crises was a norm of parliamentary supremacy.

Yet as Roger Congleton argues, parliamentary supremacy and the size of the franchise are very different things.[16] Parliament has an obvious interest seeking power for itself. It is much less obvious why it would support the extension of the franchise. Certainly members who had enjoyed the support of their rotten boroughs would want to protect that limited electorate. It is entirely possible to have a parliament with great authority backed by a very limited suffrage, or a parliament with little authority backed by universal suffrage. Bruce Bueno de Mesquita and Alastair Smith emphasise how important it is for rulers to keep the number of influential electors low—the spoils of power are better when their distribution is concentrated among a few people. Yet between the Glorious Revolution and the early twentieth century voter eligibility had gone from a tiny slice of the population to universality. So why did parliament expand its own franchise, when adding more to the franchise diluted those who had existing privilege?

Every group has an interest in influencing the political system. However in a democratic system those without suffrage are precisely those who have the least economic and political power. One often cited explanation for the expansion of suffrage is the threat of revolution. The existing political order may grant extensions to the franchise in order to head off violent upheaval. After all, revolution would take power away from the existing elite much more dramatically than reform, and of course increased the risk of expropriation.[17] This argument is intuitively plausible. The threat of overtaxed subjects leading to political upheaval is historically very real. The *World History of Tax Rebellions* lists hundreds of popular and aristocratic reactions to tax and tax increases.[18] But in the United Kingdom, the franchise expanded in steps. And, for instance, it was not revolutionary pressure that led to women's suffrage.

Congleton argues that the expansion of suffrage constituted a political bargain whereby interest groups cooperated for mutual benefit. The ability of each party to the bargain to negotiate in its favour changed over time due to economic and technological changes. The big change in the nineteenth century was the industrial revolution. It is no coincidence that suffrage expanded as industrialisation did. Industrialisation lowered the cost of organisation and advocacy. It concentrated individuals with aligned interests geographically. Where the working class were spread across the country working in agriculture, political organisation was virtually impossible. When that class was grouped in large industrial cities and even within large scale industrial concerns, organisation was much easier. This enhanced the political power of those groups as well as their leverage at an industrial level—a factory workforce can strike much more effectively than small scale farmers can. Hand in hand with those organisations changes came technological development that allowed the new groups to press their concerns more efficiently—most obviously the development of the newspaper industry brought about by cheaper printing.[19]

By 1830 around 10 per cent of the British population could vote. The Tories were the overwhelming beneficiaries of the existing system, as they controlled many more of the rotten and other uncontestable boroughs than their liberal Whig opponents. The Whigs therefore had a partisan interest in electoral reform. The 1831 election returned a Whig government under Prime Minister Earl Grey that had campaigned largely on the basis of electoral reform. The subsequent Reform Act, passed the next year, redrew electoral divisions, abolished dozens of seats, and created dozens more. The purpose was to standardise electoral divisions based roughly on electorate size. The 1832

bill also extended the franchise by lowering the property qualification across the country. While inflation had expanded the
number of individuals who met the forty shilling freehold
qualification fixed in the thirteenth century, the Reform Act
expanded the qualification to those who owned a wider variety
of property greater than £10, as well as granting it to individuals with a long term land lease of £50 or who paid an annual
rent greater than £50. This effectively doubled the franchise.

Further extensions in the franchise came in a series of bills
in the nineteenth and early twentieth century. The second
Reform Act was passed in 1867 and the third in 1884 and 1885.
Each time the franchise effectively doubled, lowering the property qualification further and redrawing electoral boundaries in
order to become more representative. The political calculation
for these bills was somewhat different. The 1867 act was in
part brought in by a conservative government under Benjamin
Disraeli. Congleton points out that momentum for electoral
change was such that the Tories were beginning to factor in
the interests of non-voters under the assumption they would
be eventually granted the franchise. It would not help the long
term Tory interest to have permanently alienated the mass of
the population and leave the cause of electoral reform entirely
to liberal Whigs. The 1867 reform was carefully designed to favour the Tory party at the margin. For instance, it went further
than the liberals would like by enfranchising greater number
of borough renters, who, it was believed, might tend to vote
according to the wishes of their conservative landlords.[20] The
third bill two decades later was brought by the liberal William
Gladstone. This bill increased the size of the voting population
to about 5.5 million.

As we have seen, the earliest voting rights in Britain were

political bargains for increased taxes. The relationship between tax and voting continued into the nineteenth century. It is no coincidence that the 1832 reforms came at the end of a virtual revolution in British taxation that transferred massive amounts of private wealth to the government in order to fight its continental wars.[21] The next milestone came after the First World War, in much different political circumstances to those that had prevailed during the nineteenth century. In 1918 the Representation of the People Act brought about near universal male suffrage and began to introduce—subject to a number of qualifications—female suffrage. In 1928 the Equal Franchise Act made female suffrage equivalent to male suffrage.

It is not well appreciated how connected female suffrage was to questions of taxation. When the fight for women's suffrage began in earnest in the latter decades of the nineteenth century, the catchcry was cribbed from the American revolution: 'no taxation without representation'. Many of the most militant suffragettes expressed their radicalism by refusing to pay taxes, and much liberal opinion was likewise turned to the cause by the unjustness of requiring women to pay taxes yet denying them the vote.

As one historian of the British suffrage movement has written, 'Tax resistance formed an important part of suffragettes' overall strategy to reject the legal obligations of women who lacked representation, drawing upon an older tradition of tax resistance in England for its authority.'[22] Tax resistance was the longest running and most political powerful weapon the suffragettes had. Between 1906 and 1918 more than 220 women became prominent tax resisters. Most of these women were drawn from the middle class.[23] One supporter of suffrage wrote in 1911 that:

altogether apart from the very valuable object lesson and warning which it presents to members of Parliament, tax-resistance is good propaganda, because it presents one of the straightest and most concise arguments for Woman's Suffrage by which we are able to reach the public conscience and arouse the indifferent. It is so simple and so direct, and nowhere have I seen any real attempt to meet it. When Anti-Suffragists tell us that the Parliament vote 'lies outside the woman's function' reduced to its bare skeleton what does that statement mean? That it is the woman's function and duty to pay money to the State for the making and maintenance of laws which affect her life, her home, and the conditions under which she earns her living just as much as they affect men; but it is not her 'function' to say how that money is to be applied, or to control the conditions of its expenditure.[24]

The Roman orator Cicero called taxes the 'sinews of the state'—the fibres that tie governments together. Taxes are also the main way the state is tied to the citizenry. The power to confiscate is the state's first power. Without it, the institutions of a state cannot support itself, let alone provide the rents or public goods that the ruler of that state needs to distribute to maintain their power. In his book *For Good and Evil*, Charles Adams makes the compelling argument that taxes are one of the primary movers of historical change—so many events in human history were driven by state overreach on taxation or the natural human desire to avoid being taxed.[25]

This chapter has focused on the history of the franchise in Britain for two reasons: it is in Britain that the institutions and ethos of liberal democracy developed, and in which we can see the long historical trajectory of social bargaining by which it did so. As a British colony, Australia owes much to this history for its franchise. Yet it was also relatively free from the established interests which made suffrage-extension such a slow, political process. When self-government was granted to the colonies of New South Wales, Victoria, South Australia and Tasmania over the second half of the nineteenth century, each instituted full suffrage for males over the age of 21—a universality which was not achieved in the mother country until after the First World War. Likewise, women's suffrage was achieved earlier in Australia than Britain. The antipodean arguments were similar to that in the home country. One Australian suffragette asked 'Should not those who had their property taxed have a voice in the representation of the taxpayers?'[26] On the eve of federation both Western Australia and South Australia granted the vote to women, and the 1902 Commonwealth Franchise Act enabled female suffrage at the federal level.

One longstanding issue in the Australian franchise has been the political status of Aboriginal people. The universal male suffrage introduced in the colonies did not distinguish between migrants and Aboriginal people. All people on the Australian continent were considered British subjects. At the first moment of democratic self-government, Australian Aboriginal people had the vote. The situation changed however with the advent of federation, an era when notions of 'White Australia' began to dominate the public mindset. Section 41 of the new Commonwealth constitution said that all adults who had the right to vote in state elections would have the right to vote federally. This provision was in large part designed to ensure that the women in South Australia who had achieved suffrage would not be denied it by the new federation. However, the rights of Aboriginal people to the vote were being wound back—in Queensland and Western Australia they had been banned from voting. The Commonwealth's 1902 franchise legislation said that 'No aboriginal native of Australia, Asia, Africa or the islands of the Pacific, except New Zealand, shall be entitled to have his name placed on the electoral roll', and Section 41 was read to give the vote only to those Aboriginal people who had already had their name on a state electoral role prior to 1901. Given that there had been little awareness by Indigenous people of their rights as British citizens during the nineteenth century this represented a tiny cohort of voters.

It was only until after the Second World War that Aboriginal Australians began to claw back their franchise. The Commonwealth Electoral Act 1949 gave the vote to Indigenous people who been in the military. It was not until 1962 that Aboriginal people were given full voting rights. (The much-praised 1967 Commonwealth referendum was not addressed to the right to vote, but to whether Aboriginal people should be included in the census—Section 127 of the Constitution explicitly excluded them from this statistical measure—and whether the federal parliament could write special laws with respect to Aboriginal people, a power which was until that time a state power.)

Australia is an exceptional democracy. It was colonised and granted self-government at a time when the democratic compact was in its greatest flux in the United Kingdom. John Hirst makes the point that developments in democratic reform in Britain set the context for decisions in Australia about democracy. The defeat of the Chartists—a British movement for democratic rights with a working class base—in 1848 cleared the ground for the middle class, incremental, democratic reformers in Britain and Australia alike.[27] This enthusiasm for political equality has to be contrasted with the shamefully protracted process by which Aboriginal people got the vote.

The history of the franchise illustrates how democracy developed as a bargain between ruler and ruled. It is too much to describe this, as some scholars do, as a form of mutual cooperation for public projects. That is too much a panglossian view of historical change. It obscures an enormous amount of violence, tyranny, confiscation and oppression. At first instance, the state relies on its coercive power in order to tax the population. It does not immediately require the consent of that population to do so. Sheer brutality can give a ruler a long and rich life at the expense a vast number of people.

But history demonstrates that sheer brutality cannot sustain a government forever. Those states which rely solely on force for their legitimacy have, over time, proven to be increasingly unstable. Technological change and public ideology have given the population a greater desire and ability to resist what it sees as excessive or oppressive government. In the long run no government can expropriate its citizens without establishing a process whereby that expropriation is legitimised by the citizens themselves. The expansion of the franchise goes hand in hand with the expansion of the tax base. Money-hungry rulers have needed to trade away some of their own power in order to expand their tax revenue. The population has demanded public goods—investment in public infrastructure, for instance, the welfare state, or just the spoils of conquest—in return for that revenue.

The previous chapter offered a social contract theory of government. The social contract is an ideal model—a hypothesis about the way state can relate to citizen, presented as a guide by which we can assess actually existing democracies. It is not a description of the states as they actually developed. This chapter however has presented a partial recovery of the social contract model as a description of the world as it came to be. Rather than a contract—which implies a degree of original deliberative agency—it is more accurate to imagine the modern democratic state as the result of a series of bargains between ruler and ruled. Political leadership is precarious. It is not only dependent on the support of a coalition of cronies—as in a one party dictatorship—but staving off the threat of popular revolution.

For our purposes, the great advantage overseeing democracy through such a framework is that it does not grant rulers any superhuman or superior qualities by assumption. Potentially any crony or, indeed, any member of the overall population could be a ruler. The existing political order is only maintained through negotiation and bargaining.

CHAPTER
THREE

THE WORST FORM OF GOVERNMENT

In a parliamentary debate in November 1947 Winston Churchill famously proclaimed that 'democracy is the worst form of Government except all those other forms that have been tried from time to time'. Churchill's statement has had the misfortune of entering popular culture, being stripped of context, and treated either as a throw-away witticism or an indictment on democratic politics. But his sentiment was more perceptive than history has given it credit. Churchill led the United Kingdom through almost the entire Second World War, from May 1940 to armistice in May 1945. Standing on a balcony outside the Ministry of Health on the day peace was declared in Europe, he declared to a crowd that 'This is your victory.' The crowd responded with 'No, it is yours.' Yet just two months later the British electorate sent the war victor packing. Clement Attlee's Labour party won a massive, 145 seat majority in the 1945 election. Having led the country against Adolf Hitler, Churchill was left to lead a decimated opposition.

Churchill was right. As a mechanism of collective decision-making, democracy has some problems. Any defence of democracy has to come to grips with the democracy's practical flaws. To understand why democracy is desirable we need to exclude the reasons it is not. An awareness of the problems of democracy makes its defence even stronger—that is, the democratic mindset is morally valuable even despite its limitations as a system of social choice. And those limitations are many.

Survey after survey demonstrates that voters have a serious lack of knowledge about politics and the political system. This extends to the most basic question that voters are required to answer: who would they prefer to represent their electorate in federal parliament? In the 2013 Australian Election Study only 54.4 per cent of voters could correctly name their local member of parliament. Australian data on voter ignorance is not as deep as that in the United States, where surveys have documented widespread ignorance about social trends, the nature of the political system, public policy issues and consequences.[1] Our compulsory voting system notwithstanding, there is little reason to believe Australians are substantially more informed than citizens of other liberal democracies. As one Australian survey concluded, 'by any standards, levels of political knowledge within the electorate are low'.[2]

As a result, voters rely on a few simple heuristics to determine how to vote in an election. Partisan identification is one such technique, as is the use of language. A voter who prefers small government will favour the candidates or parties whose rhetoric is peppered with concepts like 'free enterprise' or 'liberty', as opposed to the candidates who speak of 'social justice' and the 'fair go'. Indeed, ideology is itself a way to sort through the complexity. Ideology offers a way of interpreting the world and a vision of the good society that does not rely on detail for its power but on systems of thought. Voters will seek candidates who share their values rather than independently assess each party's policy in turn. In many ways, election campaigns are about signalling what motivates a candidate, rather than a competition between public policies.

The knowledge gap is if anything the least of democracy's problems. A more recent school of thought identifies challenges for human cooperation in cognitive error—that is, the problems that the human brain has in understanding the world and controlling its own thoughts. The collection of cognitive biases—patterns of thinking that are systemically wrong—that have been identified by psychologists is staggering and disheartening. And these biases have serious consequences for the operation of any political system.

Cognitive errors distort the way we relate to other individuals. We personalise events: that is, we overestimate our importance and significance in the actions of others. We assume we understand what other people are thinking more than is justified. We weigh negative information about a person more heavily than we do positive information about a person. However we weigh positive personal characteristics about ourselves more heavily than negative characteristics. We assume we understand other people better than they understand us. We assume that others' actions are more predictable than our own.

Cognitive errors are magnified when we relate to groups rather than individuals. We assume that our preferences and values are normal—that is, they are shared by the group at large. We tend to favour individuals within our group—community or nation, for instance—for preferential treatment. We consider the group we belong to as relatively heterogeneous—varied—where outsider groups are more homogenous. We blame outsider groups as a whole for the actions of individual members of those groups. We stereotype, assuming that an individual group member will have certain characteristics, despite no specific knowledge of that individual.

Cognitive errors also affect how we see events that affect us and others. For instance, hindsight bias describes the tendency to wrongly believe that we have predicted the course of events in the past; that we 'knew it all along'. We discount information that contradicts our prior beliefs while rating highly information that confirms it. We overrate low but highly prominent risks while discounting less prominent but more likely dangers. We prefer to protect ourselves against losses than acquiring gains. We prefer the status quo to uncertain change. These biases are responsible for some highly undesirable social phenomena. The most obvious are those that come as a result of our natural tendency to categorise the social world into groups and favour those inside our groups. Other errors make us unjustifiably risk averse, holding back otherwise desirable change.

So what do these cognitive biases mean for democratic politics? Each has an effect on our political preferences and the way we engage with the system of democracy. Some have helpful social functions. The status quo bias mitigates against some of the other cognitive errors—for instance, preventing the systemic overestimation of our understanding of the world becoming an over-confidence that we know how to engineer changes to that world. The negativity effect, which describes how humans tend to rate negative information about another person higher than positive information, can explain, for instance, why negative political advertisements are effective, or why people who have been in the public eye for a long time are more controversial or disliked than 'cleanskins' who have been prominent for a shorter period of time.

In his book *The Myth of the Rational Voter: Why Democracies Choose Bad Policies*, Bryan Caplan identifies fours systemic biases in voter policy preferences.[3] Caplan's method is to compare the views of economists—that is, experts in economic policy—with the economic views of the population. The biases he identifies are the antimarket bias, the antiforeign bias, the pessimistic bias, and the make-work bias. Thanks to the antimarket bias, voters systemically underestimate the economic benefits of markets. They are hostile to foundational economic concepts like interest and see monopolies where there are none. They prefer to discipline the social order through direct government regulation rather than the constraints of competitive markets.

The antiforeign bias describes the tendency to 'underestimate the benefits of interaction with foreigners'. This of course is a reflection of some of the most tribal underpinnings of the human relationships. It manifests itself in hostility to immigration and a preference for tariffs and quotas over free trade. The success of the free trade movement over the last few decades has been in spite of this innate desire to build economic barriers against the world.

The pessimistic bias describes the tendency of voters to heavily weight negative forecasts of the future and underweight positive ones. The long-term trajectory of the Western world since the industrial revolution has been one of unprecedented growth in living standards and wealth. Along almost every indicator humanity has enjoyed sustained improvement. Nevertheless, population surveys demonstrate that voters are pessimistic about the future, concerned by ominous economic forecasts and portents of impending decline.

Finally, the make-work bias means that voters tend to favour policies that increase the demand for labour above all other factors. This means that economic activity is praised for how many jobs it creates rather than the value it brings. As Caplan points out, the crudest form of make-work bias is Luddism, the belief that technology 'takes' jobs and therefore, despite the obvious benefits technology brings, is a net cost to human welfare. The make-work bias systemically understates the social benefits of shifting labour into more profitable fields.

And yet, knowledge problems, foundational cognitive biases and systemically wrong policy preferences go only part of the way to describing the problems with democracy. Even if voters were not afflicted by these cognitive errors—that is, even if we assume perfect voters—there is no reason to believe those ideal preferences will be translated by the democratic system into ideal policy.

Representative democracy is one great 'agency problem'. Voters ('principals') want their elected leaders to represent their interests and political preferences within the machinery of state. Yet those representative ('agents') respond to incentives like everybody else, and there are few inbuilt structural incentives to ensure that the agents are working in the interests of the principals. In the principal-agent relationship, agents have their own preferences about their own action, and will pursue those preferences to the extent that their liberty allows.

Agency problems are manifest in much human cooperative endeavour. Businesses resolve the principal-agent problem that characterises the employer-employee relationship with positive and negative incentives. At the simplest level, employers monitor the activity and work of their employees, and terminate the employment of those employees who stray too far from the principal's preferences. More sophisticated techniques such as commissions and profit sharing are attempts to align the agents' incentives with the principals'.

In representative democracy elections are supposed to align the interests of the agents with that of the principals. Elections first offer elected representatives a mandate: successful election legitimises their future actions in parliament or government. Once elected they duly and rightly can perform state functions. Second, elections offer a negative incentive—a threat—to ensure those functions are performed in the interests of the voters. Representatives who fail to satisfy the demands of electors risk losing at the next election.[4]

It would not do to underestimate fear of electoral loss in our contemporary politicians. But an election is a weak mechanism to resolve the principal agent problem. Elections are extremely rare. Voters are typically offered a limited choice of candidates—in Australia we have four major parties, Liberal, Labor, National, and Green—not all of whom will run in each seat. (Party affiliation is important because it signals that the candidates have gone through a previous formal selection process to assure candidate quality.) In one prominent model, the key to controlling elected politicians is widespread agreement in the electorate on standards of performance, which can be applied retrospectively to incumbents.[5] This agreement of course does not exist.

Furthermore, measuring whether political candidates achieve what they had promised to do is inherently difficult. Political candidates usually try to give themselves wiggle room to vary their future action and avoid making overly declarative statements. As the economist Robin Hanson has pointed out, if politicians that really want to demonstrate they plan to keep their promises, they would post bonds that would be forfeit if those promises were broken.[6] Of course they do not. A 2009 overview of research into election promises tentatively found that political parties across Europe and the United States keep just two-thirds of their promises.[7] If anything, this seems high. Centuries of experience with democracy have conditioned us to be cynical about the trustworthiness of politicians. But a two-thirds success rate of keeping explicit promises is well below the standard we would expect from, for instance, an employee or contractor.

Agency theory puts a different perspective on Edmund Burke's famous and highly-praised 1774 speech to the electors of Bristol. Burke argued:

> Parliament is not a congress of ambassadors from different and hostile interests; which interests each must maintain, as an agent and advocate, against other agents and advocates; but parliament is a deliberative assembly of one nation, with one interest, that of the whole; where, not local purposes, not local prejudices, ought to guide, but the general good, resulting from the general reason of the whole. You choose a member indeed; but when you have chosen him, he is not member of Bristol, but he is a member of parliament.[8]

This speech is a signal that the principal-agent incentives are radically out of alignment. Burke explicitly rejects the model of representation and treats his election more as a legitimation of his appointment to a state aristocracy. In his view, voters ought not to expect to be 'represented' per se by his actions in parliament, but they ought to expect he will merely be guided by his own conscience.

Bristol voters would have been right to be displeased. Burke's defiant speech was given immediately after he was elected in the general election in November 1774. This was his first time representing that constituency. After a controversial term in parliament, where his support of free trade with Ireland and Catholic Emancipation put him offside with his Bristol support base, Burke was tossed out at the next general election in 1780, coming last of five candidates. Burke had followed his conscience, and Bristol voters had to wait six years to impose control on their 'representative'.

So elections are highly imperfect mechanisms to overcome principal-agent problems. What makes them worse is that from the perspective of an individual voter it doesn't make much sense to invest the time and energy into monitoring and assessing the political performance of their local representative. Australian federal divisions for the House of Representatives have around 90,000 to 100,000 electors. A single vote, no matter how informed that vote may be, is extremely unlikely to sway that election. In the United States, a survey of 56,613 separate Congressional and state legislature elections could find only 10 that were reported to have come down to a single vote—that is, where there was a 'pivotal vote' that determined the election outcome. Of those 10, recounts found that they were in fact won by a larger margin.[9] (Counting votes is not an exact science and mistakes are extremely common.)

Caplan argues that voters are therefore 'rationally irrational'.[10] Voters realise that their individual votes are not going to determine the outcome of an election. They have little incentive to get informed or to develop mechanisms to constrain their representatives. Voting is an act of expression rather than a mechanism of preference alignment. While public policy can have serious effects on the lives of individual voters—by raising or lowering economic wellbeing, for instance—those individual voters are unable to effectively influence that public policy through the voting mechanism. Thus the returns to acquiring new knowledge about policy and the political system are quite low. The four systemic policy biases Caplan identifies are the result of this rational irrationality—there is simply little incentive for voters to overcome those biases. For instance, biases favouring in-groups over out-groups can be happily indulged at the ballot box because voting is merely expressive.

We have collected here a rather dispiriting pyramid of problems with democracy. First, voters have vastly different capabilities. Second, even if they had equal capability, there are too many areas of government responsibility—too many policies and alternatives—for any one voter to comprehend. Third, even if voters were capable of engaging with all that government does, they are afflicted by a large number of cognitive biases and errors that undermine their decision making capabilities. These manifest themselves in systemically wrong policy preferences. Fourth, even if voters had optimal policy preferences, the endemic principal agent problems in modern democratic systems gives them little control over their elected representatives to pursue those preferences. These problems of course do not operate in isolation: they interact and intertwine to sometimes offset and sometimes exacerbate democratic failure.

Winston Churchill's statement about democracy being the worst form of government has come down to us in history as little more than a quip; an aphorism that he must have seen at the time as disposable but appealed to enough compilers of quotation books that it has now stuck in the historical memory. Never is it made clear what Churchill meant by democracy— and what was the nature of the 'other forms' of government he was referring to. Yet as the full quote makes clear, it was not the twin menaces of fascism or communism that he was worrying about, but rule by experts:

> All this idea of a handful of men getting hold of the State machine, having the right to make the people do what suits their party and personal interests or doctrines, is complete-ly contrary to every conception of surviving Western de-mocracy ... All this idea of a group of super men and su-per-planners, such as we see before us, 'playing the angel,' as the French call it, and making the masses of the people do what they think is good for them, without any check or correction, is a violation of democracy.
>
> Many forms of Government have been tried, and will be tried in this world of sin and woe. No one pretends that democracy is perfect or all-wise.
>
> Indeed, it has been said that democracy is the worst form of Government except all those other forms that have been tried from time to time; but there is the broad feel-ing in our country that the people should rule, continuously rule, and that public opinion, expressed by all constitutional means, should shape, guide, and control the actions of Min-isters who are their servants and not their masters.[11]

As Churchill said this, the Labor Prime Minister Clement Attlee was working to transform Britain along socialist lines. Attlee laid the foundations for the massive British welfare state and its nationalised health service. His program of national-isation ultimately bought a fifth of the British economy into public ownership. This program would ultimately give Britain the sclerotic economy that Margaret Thatcher had to deal with 40 years later.

The Attlee reforms bought an army of administrators and reformers into the machinery of government. An economy driven by entrepreneurs became an economy managed by bureaucrats. It was this transfer of power—from the population to experts—that Churchill contrasted with democracy. Churchill believed that the people should 'shape, guide, and control' the government, not a cadre of elite technocrats. And it is this relationship—between experts and democracy—that we turn to in the next chapter.

CHAPTER

FOUR

THE CULT OF EXPERTISE

In his book *Hatred of Democracy*, the French philosopher Jacques Rancière contrasts the method by which the ancient Greeks chose those who ran the state with the modern system of representative democracy.[1] Athenian democracy drew lots to allocate government roles—a decision making technique known to political theorists as 'sortition'. In effect the institutions of government were populated by random chance. At first the drawing of the lot involved picking beans from a container. Later in the life of Athenian democracy special devices, *kleroteria*, were used to allocate roles.[2] Almost every Athenian public office was filled by sortition: magistrates, bureaucrats, the police, and administrators were all chosen by random chance.

Likewise, the 500 person jury that sat in court judgment was also filled by lot. The only office that was not filled by sortition was the military leadership. Generals were popularly elected.

Unfortunately, we know less about how the system worked than we would like. The historian Peter Liddel raises some of the main questions: were lots drawn from all eligible citizens or just those who volunteered? In other words: where the offices of state filled coercively? Liddel argues that the evidence suggests that participation in the Assembly—the other pillar of Athenian democracy by which public policy decisions were decided—was likely voluntary. There is some evidence that low rates of volunteering necessitated payment for participation.[3]

Sortition is a challenging concept. It seems to reject one of the foundational beliefs of our modern age: meritocracy. Many people believe that democracy at its best is a mechanism to sort the wheat from the chaff. It is supposed to allow societies to choose the best leaders from among the population: the most capable, the most intelligent, the most politic. Sortition seems to reject this. As one nineteenth century scholar wrote,

> There is no institution of ancient history which is so difficult of comprehension as that of electing officials by the lot. We have ourselves no experience of the working of such a system; any proposal to introduce it now would appear so ludicrous that it requires some effort for us to believe that it ever did prevail in a civilised community.[4]

There is good reason for our incomprehension. Rancière argues that when the Athenians drew lots they were undermining the final form of hierarchy by which free citizens could be divided and ranked—that of 'competence'. Human societies have always been ranked by family and birth-order or brute strength. When democracies opened public positions up to elections and extending the franchise, they eliminated the hierarchies of nobility and force. But they left one final 'title' by which humans could be ranked, that of knowledge and competence: 'the authority of those who know over those who are ignorant.'

In Athens, electors were prevented from choosing the most virtuous, or intelligent, or suave, or cunning among their ranks for office. The flipside of this was that those who won positions in government were under no illusion where their legitimacy came from. Sortition prevented those in power from harbouring any sense that they were especially worthy of their responsibilities.

Ours is an age of expertise. We in the twenty-first century are the heirs of great learning of the past. We benefit from the knowledge and understanding of centuries. But there's a big difference between recognising and respecting that knowledge and elevating expertise beyond the realm of learning and into the political domain. Today, expertise is no longer used to make positive assessments—that is, to describe the world as it is—but to make normative judgements—to describe the world as it could be rearranged. Three centuries on from the Enlightenment, science and rationality are not just principles to guide our understanding of the world around us but principles on which the social order is constructed.

The purpose of this chapter is to examine expertise and competence in Rancière's sense and to ultimately reject it as the basis for governing. The existence of expertise, and differing levels of intellectual capability, is no challenge to the political and moral equality that underpins democracy. Indeed, a close examination of expertise ought to enhance an appreciation of that fundamental egalitarianism. In this chapter we necessarily talk in the abstract. In later chapters we shall go into some detail about how expertise has been embedded in our political system in an undemocratic way—institutionally, through the removal of some bureaucracies from the chains of democratic accountability, and ideologically, through the paternalistic assumptions that citizens ought to have their choices and options limited or manipulated for their own good.

But first it must be admitted that as a system of governance, expertise has some obvious appeal. The previous chapter demonstrated the many deficiencies of the existing democratic form. Many of those are rooted in voter ignorance—rational or otherwise. Complaints about the ignorance of the masses are an ancient theme in anti-democratic thought. The 'Old Oligarch', an anonymous writer in ancient Greece, complained of democratic Athens that it had 'given the advantage to the vulgar people at the expense of the good'. The Old Oligarch argued that the poverty of the lower orders made them unworthy of the high responsibility of democratic participation:

> in the people ... we find a very high degree of ignorance, disorder, and vileness; for poverty more and more leads them in the direction of bad morals, thus also the absence of education and in the case of some persons the ignorance which is due to the want of money.[5]

Two millennia later, a group of barristers shortly before the French Revolution echoed the Old Oligarch's beliefs when they wrote:

> Whatever respect one might wish to show for the rights of humanity in general, there is no denying the existence of a class of men who, by virtue of their education and the type of work to which their poverty had condemned them, is ...

incapable at the moment of participating fully in public affairs.[6]

With democracy crippled by ignorance and self-interest, surely, it has long been reasoned, that a solution would be to engage those who are not ignorant—that is, those who are expert—in the formation of public policy. In an influential essay published in 1887, the future president of the United States Woodrow Wilson wrote of the need for a science of administration to guide benevolent bureaucrats opposing, where necessary, popular democratic preferences. Describing the vast majority of people as 'selfish, ignorant, timid, stubborn, or foolish', Wilson called for an elite corps of the wise to head up the operations of government. Public opinion was not to be ignored, but weighed, and if necessary, guided.

> The problem is to make public opinion efficient without suffering it to be meddlesome. Directly exercised, in the oversight of the daily details and in the choice of the daily means of government, public criticism is of course a clumsy nuisance, a rustic handling delicate machinery.[7]

The political theorist Robert Dahl describes this sort of political system as 'guardianship'—an alternative to democracy where the rulers and decision-makers constitute 'a minority of persons who are specially qualified by reason of their superior knowledge and virtue.'[8]

The purest expression of the guardianship model of government appears in Plato's *Republic*. In this book, Plato describes a utopian society, *kallipolis* or the 'beautiful state', as a way to describe what a just state would look like and to describe how individuals ought to act in an ideal world. So who should rule the beautiful state—the competent or the incompetent? Through the words of Socrates, Plato asked,

> Inasmuch as philosophers only are able to grasp the eternal and unchangeable, and those who wander in the region of the many and variable are not philosophers, I must ask you which of the two classes should be the rulers of our State?[9]

In Plato's argument, only philosophers, with their disinterested love of knowledge, were capable of ruling. Philosophers had both the understanding of justice and the knowledge of statecraft in order to maximise prosperity, eliminate poverty, and promote virtue. Plato was as opposed to hereditary monarchy and aristocracy—that is, hierarchy by birth—as he was democracy—hierarchy by popularity, or, in the Athenian sense, hierarchy by random chance. Philosopher-kings derived their legitimacy by the virtue of their deep wisdom.

It is easy to dismiss Plato's ancient reasoning as anachronistic. Since his time we have suffered through centuries of authoritarianism that ought to make most sceptical about any authoritarian political model, regardless of what basis that authoritarianism is justified. From our vantage point—and perhaps the vantage point of many readers in Ancient Greece—the *kallipolis* looks more like a dystopian nightmare than an ideal state. Karl Popper famously described Plato as a proto-fascist, whose ideal society was totalitarianism.[10] In the *kallipolis*, families and monogamous sexual relations would be abolished and women made into communal property, the unfit would be left to die, and there would be censorship of poetry and other art. Furthermore, the economic redistribution needed to eliminate poverty would be repressive.

Nevertheless, the fact that the specifics of Plato's guardianship proposal are repellent has done little to undermine his broader philosopher-king ideal. The idea that experts could take control of the institutions of power to direct states in a social optimal fashion is a highly seductive one. It speaks to longstanding dissatisfaction with the 'messiness' of democratic governance.

And of course there are no greater supporters of rule by experts than the experts themselves. For all those who hold a strong and clear vision of an ideal social order, or just a keen sense of what ills the current order, democracy can be strikingly inconvenient. For instance, in their 2007 book *The Climate Change Challenge and the Failure of Democracy*, two Australian academics, David Shearman and Joseph Wayne Smith, argue that democracy and liberalism have been unable to tackle climate change and protect the environment, and therefore

> there is some merit in the idea of a ruling elite class of philosopher kings. These are people of high intellect and moral virtue who are trained in a wide number of disciplines, ecology, the sciences, and philosophy (especially ethics), for the purpose of dealing with the crisis of civilization. Their goal will not be knowledge for its own sake, but knowledge in the service of life on earth. These new philosopher kings or ecoelites will be as committed to the value of life as the economic globalists are to the values of money and greed.[11]

Shearman and Smith argue that democracy ought to be supplanted by an authoritarian technocracy. Not the authoritarianism, apparently, of Adolf Hitler and Joseph Stalin, but a benign, Platonic authoritarianism, ruled by a meritocratic elite who are driven by the acquisition of wisdom for a specific purpose: resolving the social and environmental ills that plague humanity. (Shearman and Smith have a particular disdain for the freedom of academics in current universities to research what and however they please: for them a 'Real University' would direct socially valuable scientific research and produce consensus statements on scientific issues.) Rarely are proposals for philosopher-kings to replace democratic deliberation stated so explicitly. Shearman and Smith at least deserve credit for that. The book is a litany of complaints about the 'cult of consumerism' and how economic growth and the market economy placate the masses. It is easy to see the distaste of the vulgar citizenry underpinning their analysis: democracy is supposed to be rule by the masses but the masses have been corrupted by 'cultural materialism'.

Nevertheless, the ideal of expert-led governance needs to be taken on its own terms. It is vulnerable to one simple fact: experts and philosopher-kings are as much specimens of humanity as those they would seek to rule. In other words, even before we consider the perverse incentive structures facing political rulers, there is much reason to doubt that philosopher-kings are, in fact, the paragons of disinterested expertise that Plato and his followers would hope. Expertise only slightly mitigates the first problem identified in the previous chapter (the extreme complexity of modern democratic governance) and does nothing reduce to the second—the mass of cognitive errors and systemic biases that afflict all human decision making.

The well-known Dunning-Kruger effect demonstrates the tendency of incompetent people to be unaware of their own incompetence and unable to recognise competence in others. In other words, ignorance is no barrier to confidence; rather, ignorance can sustain it. This has been interpreted by some to be a critical problem with democracy itself.[12]

But experts are as susceptible to cognitive errors as the rest of us. There is a vast literature on expert judgement. Its results are sobering. While experts are more knowledgeable, they are also more vulnerable to biases that stem from that high level of knowledge. Expertise brings its own cognitive errors.

To start, experts are as susceptible to over-estimating their own competence as non-experts. The Dunning-Kruger effect has been observed in the very place it ought to be least likely to manifest itself: within the scholarly peer review process. Peer review, the practice of anonymous or semi-anonymous evaluation by other scholars of scholarly work before its publication, is supposed to be the gold standard of intellectual quality control. It is designed explicitly to prevent the sort of mis-evaluations of competence that the Dunning-Kruger effect describes do not occur. Experts are typically experts in narrow fields—and, with the specialisation of the modern academy, increasingly so. However, the peer review system encourages them to act as reviewers outside the narrow band of their specialty.

In truth the world is not divided into competents and in-competents, or experts and non-experts. Those who are competent in one field may be incompetent in many others. Expertise is highly bounded. Yet experts do not often recognise their own limitation when they work outside those bounds. As one discussion of this phenomenon put it,

> In the grander scheme of our scientific endeavor the Dunning-Kruger effect and the self-fulfilling prophecy of the echo-chamber create a tacit culture of collective self-deception that can dramatically narrow the diversity of scientific publications.[13]

The Dunning-Kruger effect has been found in many spheres—after all, expertise is not limited to the realm of scholarship. For instance, a study of police drivers found that expert drivers were just as likely to over-estimate their own expertise as novice drivers were.[14]

The diversity of expertise is also a critical problem if we are trying to construct a system of governance built around experts. After all, governance is, itself, a highly heterogeneous activity. One of the problems identified by the discussion on peer review is the struggle that editors have in choosing the appropriate reviewers. Editors are not necessarily experts in the topics that they publish. Governments that seek to engage the best experts to tackle a policy issue inevitably have this problem as well: how to determine who those experts are. For lay-rulers defining the terms of a debate are hard enough, let along navigating an ocean wilderness of expert opinion.

The Dunning-Kruger effect is hardly the only psychological limitation facing experts. A huge problem for expertise is overconfidence. Expert overconfidence has been heavily studied in the last few decades, in large part because the implications are so substantial. One of the key works on psychological biases argues that 'no problem in judgment and decision making is more prevalent and more potentially catastrophic than overconfidence.'[15]

The most common method to test overconfidence is described as 'calibration', a test to determine how well experts' estimations of the probability of uncertain values relate to the true occurrence of those values. If, for instance, an expert proclaims that they are 90 per cent confident of an occurrence, then out of 100 separate observations we would expect 90 of those observations to be correct. If fewer than 90 are correct then the expert is overconfident. The 'surprise index' refers to how overconfident they are—the spread between their estimates and reality. If an estimate is 90 per cent and the actual value only appears in 80 per cent of cases, then the surprise index is 10 per cent, or ten percentage points. The spread can be worryingly high: 'typical values of the surprise index range from 20 to 45%, with some values as low as 5% or over 50% being observed'.[16]

Some experts—like weather forecasters—perform better in calibration than others, thanks to their accumulated experience of getting things wrong. However, there is no consistent evidence to suggest that experts perform better on calibration studies than non-experts. Rather, the surprise index lowers when tasks and assessments are simplest. They skyrocket with complex tasks. And, as one study puts it, complex and difficult tasks are 'exactly the type of situation[s] in which expert opinion is most likely to be used'.[17]

Calibration studies are necessarily performed in experimental settings rather than the real world. Looking at real world expertise, the psychologist Philip Tetlock's magisterial book *Expert Political Judgment* found widespread error in forecasting by experts making political and policy assessments. After an enormous study involving 284 experts making more than 82,000 forecasts over 20 years, Tetlock found enormous variation between prediction and reality. A little bit a knowledge went a long way, but too much knowledge was counterproductive. Experts were little better than lay people at making forecasts but were much more confident when they did. In other words, expertise contributed to overconfidence rather than mitigated it. As he wrote,

> In this age of academic hyperspecialization, there is no reason for supposing that contributors to top journals—distinguished political scientists, area study specialists, economists, and so on—are any better than journalists or attentive readers of the New York Times in 'reading' emerging situations.[18]

These are biases that directly undermine the very benefits which expertise is supposed to bring to governance. Of course experts are as susceptible to other biases described in the previous chapter as well. Experts are no less capable of seeing past ingroup-outgroup distinctions than non-experts, no less susceptible to personalising or projecting themselves onto their understanding of the world, and no more or less vulnerable to hindsight bias or poor understandings of relative risk. One of the findings of calibration studies is that experts in calibration—who know the pervasiveness of overconfidence—themselves overcompensated for this knowledge by providing under-confident estimations.[19] It is hard to avoid humanity's psychological ticks, no matter how smart or informed you are.

Why does this matter? Public policy development is almost entirely about forecasting. It involves assessments of a likely future—often called as the 'business-as-usual' forecast—and then an alternative future determined by public policy intervention. For instance, at the start of the Global Financial Crisis of 2007-2009, governments around the world were faced with the question of what the economy would look like without substantial public policy intervention and what it would look like with that intervention. Of course, there was more than one possible intervention available to them. This was the sort of public policy conundrum where expertise was most demanded—to advise governments when it was most necessary of the proper course of action, based on a complex and highly specialised area of economic scholarship. Yet experts failed to present their democratic masters with accurate forecasts of the consequences of their policy choices.

The most prominent example of forecasting failure around the crisis was the estimates of unemployment made by the

Obama administration as part of its February 2009 stimulus package. Christina Romer, chair of the administration's peak economics body, the Council of Economic Advisors and a professor of economics, and Jared Bernstein, Vice-President Joe Biden's chief economics advisor, forecast that in the absence of a stimulus package unemployment would reach nine per cent in 2010.[20] The stimulus package would hold unemployment at just eight per cent. However in reality, even with the stimulus package, unemployment reached 10 per cent in October 2009. It was forecast to reduce to five per cent under both scenarios by the first quarter of 2014. Yet as of March 2014 it was still up around 6.7 per cent.

This forecasting error was both substantial and consequential. The unemployment estimates were used as a negotiating tool to convince Congress of the need for the Obama stimulus package. The document which contained the chart did acknowledge the underlying uncertainty that characterised the American economy in February 2009. There was also a footnote on the chart itself acknowledging the variety forecasts of unemployment rates without action ('Some private forecasters anticipate unemployment rates as high as 11%'). Romer and Bernstein were, and are, serious and respected figures. Yet despite these caveats, the belief that they could meaningfully forecast the unemployment rate—let alone the unemployment rate after an as-yet unlegislated stimulus package—five years out was obvious nonsense.

So why was it offered? In politics, arguments that rest on too much uncertainty are frail. It is much more powerful to present decision makers with a firm prediction of the future, and (perhaps more importantly) a firm prediction of what will occur if those decision makers fail to pursue a certain course of action. Political incentives in times of crisis favour drastic action—no politician wants to be blamed for failing to act on advice. The unemployment graph, regardless of how many footnotes and caveats were placed around it, provided policymakers with the false certainty they needed. Expertise has a powerful rhetorical effect. People are more likely to accept a course of action if it has been approved by recognised experts.

In this way, expert overconfidence is multiplied by the political system—experts supply overconfidence and decision makers demand overconfidence. Tetlock observed that the forecast error was most common among experts with public profiles. The logic of politics favoured those who made bold and certain claims about the uncertain future over those who hedged their bets or admitted potential error.

Cognitive biases are omnipresent but somehow we manage to survive. There are two key mechanisms by which we can mitigate those biases. The first is repetition. By making predictions repeatedly we adjust our expectations over time. The second is incentive alignment.

Unfortunately, in the real world of government, experts are never offered the change to do-over. While repetition has been shown to be a powerful tool against overconfidence in experimental games, it is the nature of public policy that most new challenges are sufficiently distinct from previous challenges that the learning by repetition is not possible. Romer and Bernstein were not offered the opportunity to replay February 2009 over and over in order to hone their unemployment forecast, or the degree of confidence with which they made them.

A more useful mechanism to mitigate inherent cognitive biases is aligning participants' incentives so that they personally bear the costs of failure. The talking head pundits who make systemically wrong predictions are able to continue to do so because they are not asked to answer for their errors in the future. The benefits of making wild guesses are high—good television—and the costs of errors virtually non-existent. This observation has led to some calls for experts to place bets on their predictions, similar to the political promise bonds proposed by Robin Hanson, and to encourage the development of betting markets for political predictions.

The political sphere does have an incentive system for mitigating error—periodic elections. The previous chapter outlined how dissatisfactory this system is. (Of course the 'pure' guardianship model—that of Plato's philosopher-king ruled *kallipolis*—would lack even the discipline of elections.) Furthermore, the consequences of poor prediction are rarely visited on those who actually make the predictions. It is politicians who are vulnerable to losing their job at an election, rather than the experts that advise them. It is not Christina Romer and Jared Bernstein who bear the consequences of their failed predictions, but—in theory—Barack Obama. Yet the number of other factors voters had to take into account when deciding whether to grant Obama a second term of the presidency would have dwarfed the crime of accepting a bad prediction from his staff. In other words, their inaccurate prediction was nearly costless—at least for them.

We have demonstrated here that experts are as vulnerable to cognitive biases and incentive misalignment as non-experts. The specific shape of those biases and incentives varies, of course, as they vary from person to person. Yet despite all this, surely we ought to prefer a government comprised of competents rather than incompetents? After all, while experts are vulnerable to overconfidence and the usual cognitive biases, they are no more so than non-experts, and at the margin must be more able to cope with the incredible intellectual challenges of government and therefore more suited for decision making.

Perhaps. But this desire for competence over incompetence overlooks the fact that the political system—any political system—favours precisely the sort of people who are expert in politics, not public affairs. Almost any system that involves the attaining and keeping of power is going to select experts in precisely that. As Rancière writes, the Athenian system of office allocated by random chance was specifically designed to avoid this:

> [T]he drawing of lots was the remedy to an evil at once much more serious and much more probable than a government of incompetents: government comprised of a certain competence, that of individuals skilled at taking power through cunning.[21]

Plato's philosopher-kings do not emerge out of nowhere. They must compete with other philosophers to obtain their high political positions. This necessity will favour philosophers who are better at competition than their competitors. Only in a system that deliberately tries to eliminate that competition is it possible to avoid the basic problem that those who seek power are the last people we would want to grant power to.

The arguments for government by random chance are uncomfortably strong. Rancière is a French critical philosopher whose biggest fan is the French Socialist Party leader Ségolène Royal. The chapter on sortition in the *Encyclopedia of Public Choice*—the standard text on the economics of politics, a field that is often seen as the domain of the liberal free market right—mounts a strong defence of sortition as a mechanism to resolve many of the most pervasive incentive problems in democratic governance.

> Sortition served well those states that used it as a collective decision making technology ... It restrains the growth of an independent political class, impedes manipulation of the political apparatus, impairs factional discord, restrains state power, protects vulnerable minorities and reduces rent-seeking. Decision methodologies incorporating some degree of randomness hold promise for addressing instances of governmental failure revealed through the public choice analysis of political institutions.[22]

The point, for our purposes, is not to here say that we ought to replace our complex system of ballots with drawing by lot, but to ask why it is such an uncomfortable idea. It is certainly no less 'democratic' than any alternative. For Aristotle, sortion was the defining characteristic of a democracy. Aristotle classed countries that used elections as aristocratic or oligarchic. Elections perpetuate rather than undermine hierarchies. They favour those who have natural advantages of wealth, power, or ability.[23] Aristotle recognised that government by election was more democratic than, say, hereditary monarchy, but democracy's purest manifestation was government by sortition.

Sortition is also challenging because it constitutes a rejection of one of the foundational beliefs of modern society: that all social challenges are reducible to a collection of scientific or engineering tasks. The Enlightenment and the subsequent Industrial Revolution inculcated the idea that resolving problems was a matter of acquiring and deploying knowledge. Plato's philosopher-king was transformed into the scientist-king or engineer-king. Government, in the popular mind, has become the art of problem solving. With that presupposition, the idea that we might allocate the job of problem solving to members of society on chance seems counterproductive, if not dangerous. There is no reason for us to believe that a randomly selected citizen would be capable of solving the thorny problems of the modern state.

But government, whether democratic or authoritarian, does not select those who are most capable at solving social problems. It selects those who are most capable at being selected for power. We might dream of rule by disinterested experts. But the result will be rule by self-interested experts—the sort of people who rise to political power.

So where does that leave us? The last two chapters have made a large number of dispiriting claims about the functioning of democracy as it is, and the functioning of a guardianship model of government. If anything the challenges to the latter have been understated. We have not, for instance, tackled the corrupting effect that power might have on even the most virtuous expert, should they be placed suddenly into office. Nor have we claimed that the virtuous expert is a chimera—an illusion dreamed up by petty despots looking to wield power themselves.

But, then, government is a human institution, and one that has to be built with human limitations in mind. Likewise, a defence of democracy has to be built around those limitations. The argument that we have presented is this: democracy is not desirable because it functions well, or efficiently. Rather, democracy is desirable to the extent that it is a system of government that recognises a fundamental human moral equality. It is desirable because it is a formal rejection of hierarchy: the hierarchy of wealth, birth, or ability. It ranks the poorest he alongside the greatest he. It grants to each member of society

THE CULT OF EXPERTISE

an equal stake in the political system, whether they choose to engage with it or not. There are no formal constraints on political or social participation under a democratic system.

Democracy, in other words, is the political manifestation of human social equality. When we say something is 'undemocratic' we are rarely referring to the formal institutions of representation and elections, but rather something that rejects that equality. In the chapters that follow we follow this logic through to its conclusions, which are far broader and far more radical than most who profess themselves to be democrats have come to terms with.

CHAPTER

FIVE

ANTI-DEMOCRATIC INSTITUTIONS

In his 2014 book the *Political Bubble: Why Australians Don't Trust Politics*, the former Labor Party leader Mark Latham offers some solutions to what he sees as Australia's democratic crisis: 'the cycle of distrust and dishonour that has turned public office into a lowly vocation'.

One of Latham's solutions is 'independent policy-making'. Latham argues that the responsibility for fiscal policy and climate change policy should be taken out of the hands of politicians and given to independent bureaucrats. The model, for Latham, is the Reserve Bank of Australia (RBA). In the same way that Australia's central bank sets interest rates without reference to parliament, so too could the controversial areas of taxation and climate change mitigation be made statutorily independent. As Latham writes,

> These [areas] tend to be difficult, contentious issues ripe for scare campaigns and political opportunism. In comprehending their technical challenges, most MPs lack appropriate tertiary qualifications. Bodies similar to the Reserve Bank could be established to frame an independent climate change strategy and determine the major features of the federal budget (such as outlay and revenue targets, appropriate deficit/surplus levels and debt management policies).[1]

There's an apparently unintended irony here. His book is purportedly about the sources of discontent with parliamentary democracy. Yet one of his solutions is to eliminate parliamentary democratic control of the most significant functions of the state.

Latham isn't the only former politician calling for politicians to exit the stage. John Hewson, leader of the federal Liberal Party between 1990 and 1994, also argues that the 'short-term-focused, adversarial policy and political environment' demands that we replicate the institutions of monetary policy for fiscal policy. What Australia needs is an independent taxation authority, 'with powers, in consultation with governments but only subject to broad parliamentary oversight, to analyse, develop, educate and deliver the reform package(s) it believes necessary over the next few decades—an RBA-type role.'[2]

The person who has spelt out this proposal in greatest detail is Nicholas Gruen, an economist who was, when he made the argument in 1997, an Assistant Commissioner with the Industry Commission, itself an independent government authority. (The Industry Commission acted in a review and advisory capacity only. Like its successor the Productivity Commission, it had no power to impose implement its recommendations.) Gruen proposed a Central Fiscal Authority, possibly integrated with the RBA, that would have the power to vary tax rates in the same way that the central bank varies interest rates. While the tax mixture—that is, the relative size of taxes like income and sales tax compared to each other—would be fixed by parliament, the absolute tax rate—how high those taxes would be—would be set by the new fiscal authority, within statutory guidelines. The authority would be guided by the level of economic activity, the budget balance, and even moral questions like intergenerational equality. In Gruen's view, this would counterbalance 'populist fiscal rectitude', where voters are unfortunately sympathetic to policies which return budgets to surplus.[3]

There are few more symbolic manifestations of our anti-democratic age than the fetishisation of 'independence'. As Latham, Hewson and Gruen demonstrate, the apparent success of the independent monetary policy managed by the RBA has provided a model for further limiting democratic control over public policy.

Yet it isn't just the RBA which has been moved outside of the usual accountability structures of representative government. Indeed, the shape of modern Australian government resembles a spider's web of autonomous and independent bureaucratic agencies whose relationship to democratically elected politicians ranges from tenuous to non-existent. The major economic regulators—the Australian Competition Consumer Commission (ACCC), the Australian Prudential Regulatory Agency (APRA), and the Australian Securities and Investment Commission (ASIC)—are statutorily independent from ministerial control. Their chief executives and commissioners are appointed by the elected government and are required to attend the occasional parliamentary committee hearing, but outside those constraints they operate independently. Likewise there are a host of other bureaucracies and organisations that jealously guard their autonomy. The most obvious are the public broadcasters, who are outside political control by tradition and practice, or bodies such as the Australian Human Rights Commission which are specifically designed to be critics of the elected government.

All these bodies act with the authority of the state—all make and influence public policy in some fashion. Regulatory agencies make policy in a literal sense, by setting regulatory guidelines and policies with the detail absent from their enabling statutory framework. The other bodies run campaigns, influence policy making, and lobby governments protected by their taxpayer support and legislative authority. So when Latham, Hewson and Gruen propose to take tax policy out of the hands of democratically elected politicians they are not proposing anything particularly radical—rather, their proposals are an obvious evolution of the drive towards regulatory and bureaucratic independence.

Central bank independence has not always been the gold standard of bureaucratic respectability. Indeed, in Australia, full central bank independence was not achieved until the election of the Howard government. In 1990 the Treasurer Paul Keating defiantly argued that he would 'not abrogate responsibility for the stance of monetary policy from the elected government to unelected and unrepresentative public officials in the name of fighting inflation first.'[4] But even at that stage the RBA had carved out more independence than it had enjoyed in previous decades. Hewson, making the case for fiscal independence, recalled sitting in a cabinet committee as a staff member of Malcolm Fraser's government listening to a group of farmers determine the interest rates and how best to intervene in exchange markets.[5] Monetary policy in that era was seen as a legitimate area of parliamentary and executive influence.

Is the independence fetish justified? The argument for independence is as follows. In the traditional Westminster bureaucratic system, the bureaucracy acts in accordance with the wishes of the minister—an elected politician drawn from the parliament. The bureaucracy is, as one Australian Royal Commission described it, 'an extension of the minister's capacity'.[6] The bureaucracy privately offers policy advice and implements policy. It does not make the final policy decisions. Yet ministers are politicians. Their interests are political. The fear is that policy decisions could be made for political reasons—as Hewson suggested, politician-farmers choosing the interest rate to favour farming interest rather than the broader interests of the economy or society. Politicians might want to make regulatory decisions on political rather than market failure grounds.

A secondary problem with political control of policy is competence. Ministers are drawn from a pool of politicians and the talent pool may be thin. Minister may not have the policy knowledge or intellectual capacity to make what are, in the modern state, extremely complex policy decisions.

In the previous chapter we cast doubt on these arguments. Regulators and bureaucrats suffer from as many cognitive biases as non-expert politicians, and are susceptible to the overconfidence that their specialty brings them. Overconfidence can be as corrupting a bias as under-expertise. Regulators are as likely to interpret events favourably for their own performance as anybody else. The economist Slaviša Tasić asks 'are regulators rational?' and concludes that:

> the input of cognitive psychology calls for a more careful approach to regulation. It points to the human fallibility, and jointly with the economics of collective decision-making, warns that government intervention is the area where such mistakes are more likely to occur than in private decisions.[7]

In practice, the actual performance of independent regulatory agencies in Australia leaves much to be desired. Australia's regulators are empire-builders—self-interested bureaucratic agencies in a contest for scarce taxpayer resources and political prominence. Plato imagined his philosopher-kings to be characterised by their notions of just and virtue. More modern arguments for expert rule rely on the 'disinterested' nature of technocrats, cocooned from the perfidy of politics. But in practice our contemporary manifestation of expert rule—that is, expert rule by independent bureaucracy—demonstrates that expertise is no panacea to error, power-seeking, mismanagement, and scandal.

For instance, the ACCC, Australia's competition and consumer regulator, has built a reputation for publicity hunger and extra-parliamentary policy making.[8] ASIC, the corporate regulator, is both heavy handed and ineffective. It is the most enthusiastic user of section 313 of the Telecommunications Act, which gives it the ability to force internet service providers to block websites. But as it admitted to a parliamentary review in 2014, it does not fully understand the mechanism by which this blocking is achieved. In the first half of 2013 ASIC 'inadvertently' blocked more than a quarter of a million websites because its enforcement team was not aware that internet protocol addresses could refer to more than one website.[9] This rather high-profile incompetence is matched by ASIC's dismal reputation at enforcing the corporate regulation it is charged with. ASIC has been criticised in court cases for being oppressive, abusing due process, and bringing the administration of justice into disrepute.[10]

Nor is the Reserve Bank the paragon of regulatory virtue that it is presented. The lack of political control has led to a crisis of accountability within the Australian regulatory community. That crisis became manifest most clearly in the Reserve Bank bank note scandal of the late 1990s and early 2000s. It is a story worth briefly telling because it illustrates that statutory independence can foster practices as perverse as any 'political' management.[11]

In 1996 the Reserve Bank founded a firm named Securency, 50 per cent owned by the bank, to produce the polymer film that constituted Australia's new plastic bank notes. Securency would make the film and another corporate body owned by the Reserve Bank, Note Printing Australia, would produce bank notes and passports. Polymer bank notes were an Australian invention, and the Reserve Bank and its subsidiaries took to selling the technology to other central banks around the world.

This is all proper, up to a point. However, one of the potential customers they had in mind was Saddam Hussein. In May 1998 Reserve Bank officials flew into Baghdad to try to negotiate a contract to sell the bank notes to the Ba'athist regime. This was problematic for a number of reasons. First, the Australian government had officially declared its intention to support military action against Saddam Hussein. On the Iraqi side of the border, Reserve Bank officers were giving a sales-pitch to

Hussein's representatives. Apparently the dictator was very impressed with the Australian product. On the Kuwaiti side of the border 190 Australian troops were preparing to attack Iraq. It would be hard to imagine an independent regulator more at odds with an elected government than that. Even worse, the Australian government had financial sanctions on Iraq at the time—sanctions that were supposed to be enforced by none other than the Reserve Bank of Australia. Internal documents released since show that the central bank understood that they were breaching the sanctions, and attempted to bypass their limits by writing contracts with the Iraqi government deliverable when the embargo was lifted.

The bank note scandal occurred at an important time in the history of the Reserve Bank, in the first few years of formal independence. The bank was also in the midst of finalising the corporatisation of Note Printing Australia, which gave that subsidiary even more independence from the political system. ASIC, too, is implicated in the bank note scandal. It failed to chase down allegations that the RBA and its subsidiaries were bribing foreign officials. The scandal occurred likewise at a critical juncture for ASIC: it was in 1998 that the corporate regulator gained its current, enlarged and empowered, form.

Of course, the fact that independent bureaucracies have shown themselves to be as perfidious as elected representatives does not demonstrate that independence is inferior to political control. Securency was a scandal, but would we really want parliament setting interest rates? Yet central bank monetary independence—even if that central bank behaves properly—does not deserve the plaudits it has received. It absolutely true that central banks have had a greater degree of success in recent decades than they have since the end of the nineteenth century gold standard. At least until the Global Financial Crisis most Western nations had enjoyed a relative price stability that previous decades had lacked. But that this success is only relatively recent however is itself suggestive of expert failure—central banks have been common for at least a century yet the experts who have managed them have been seduced by inappropriate and dangerous monetary theories and sectional interests. The monetary philosopher-kings have got many things wrong.

It is important to distinguish between two separate changes in the institutional structure of monetary policy. The trend towards independence has been accompanied by a trend towards greater rules-based monetary policy. Central banks which follow rules governing the circumstances under which monetary policy is to be eased or tighten outperform those which rely more on the discretion of their staff. It is rules-based monetary policy, rather than statutory independence, that is responsible for the greater price stability we have seen.[12]

One could plausibly argue that rules-based monetary policy is only possible when independence has been granted to central banks. The two developed parallel but not in tandem. In the case of Australia, rule following is a matter of practice rather than legislation: the statutes governing the central bank have not been altered. Rather, the rule has developed as a norm over time. The Reserve Bank Act gives the RBA an extraordinary amount of flexibility to pursue any policy settings it desires. Parliament could easily write legislation constraining the RBA to operate within an interest rate window. The choice does not have to be between bureaucratic discretion or parliamentary discretion, it can be between discretion and rules.

For politicians, bureaucratic independence is a two way street. It prevents them using the powers of the agencies to achieve their political goals. Farmer-politicians are no longer able to consistently deliver benefits to their supporters, nor take credit for those benefits when they are realised. But on the other hand, they are no longer blamed for when benefits are taken away. In the case of central banks, monetary policy can be either tight or easy, and politicians may be reluctant to impose tight policy lest it distress a key constituency. Likewise, politicians do not bear the responsibility for regulatory action against firms. Either way, regulatory independence is an abrogation of the basic responsibilities of democratic politicians. The decisions of independence agencies lack the legitimacy of decisions made by elected representatives.

This is obvious when we consider again the structure of government as a principal-agent problem. Governments derive their legitimacy from the fact that they are comprised of individuals who have been elected as representatives of the citizenry. As we have seen, this mechanism is weak but not non-existent. Bureaucracies are the arms of their minister. As one Australian public service mandarin once argued,

> Formally the Minister is the department. Without a Minister there cannot be a department. Departmental staff are appointed under Public Service Acts to discharge the functions assigned to the Minister and only to offices whose creation the Minister has endorsed. The Permanent Head is the Minister's adviser and the manager of the department's staff … And remember, Parliaments do not provide funds for Permanent Heads. Funds are provided for departments, i.e. the relevant Ministers.[13]

In practice of course the minister is not the department, no more than an employer is his employee. But it is a useful fiction. It captures the fact that while ministers may delegate certain duties to their department—the implementation of policy, or the giving of advice—the department is directly accountable to the minister for their performance of those duties. Likewise, in the Westminster system, the minister ought to be directly responsible for the performance of their department. This is a chain of delegation and accountability that leads through the public service, through the ministry and cabinet, through the parliament and ultimately back to voters.

Independent agencies are deliberately separated from this chain. While they are delegated responsibility by parliament they are not directly accountable to parliament. In a democratic system this has no justification. Under what right do regulators rule?

Supporters of regulator independence often seek to base their legitimacy on their professional competence and expertise—the apparent absence of political considerations in their decision making leaves room for purely expert-led public service. In practice their performance does not justify this anti-democratic legitimisation. The philosopher-kings of the independent bureaucracy are not as capable as their commanding role in the system of government demands.

The proposal of Latham, Hewson and Gruen for an independent fiscal body is an extreme variation of a long-developing trend within Western governments for anti-majoritarian—that is, anti-democratic—rule by bureaucracy. Their proposal is easy to pick on, of course. It would be hard to imagine any more central decision for governments to make than the appropriate level of taxation, a decision which goes to the very heart of the relationship between citizen and state. But underlying the desire for independent control of government is a belief in experts over citizens—a valorisation of expertise and a distaste for the politics that characterises a free and open democracy.

CHAPTER

SIX

Dismal equality

If Thomas Carlyle hated anything, he hated utilitarianism.
Carlyle was one of the nineteenth century's most prominent
and most influential British writers. He was utterly disdainful
of the 'pig philosophy' being promoted by the classical economists John Stuart Mill and Jeremy Bentham. Utilitarianism
advised governments to act in a way that would maximise
happiness—utility—for the maximum number of people. For
Carlyle, this was absurd; utilitarians were the most owlish of
owls, the loudest 'quacks that ever quacked'.[1]

Today Carlyle has been relegated to obscurities of literary
history, but he was as close to an intellectual superstar as that
era produced. He was friends with almost every major philoso-

pher and thinker of the times—Herman Melville, Robert Peel, Charles Dickens, Edwin Chadwick, Thomas Cooper, Ralph Waldo Emerson, just to name a few. The utilitarian Mill was among them, too. George Eliot wrote that

> there is hardly a superior or active mind of this generation that has not been modified by Carlyle's writings; there has hardly been an English book written for the last ten or twelve years that would not have been different if Carlyle had not lived.[2]

Another writer was even more certain, arguing that 'there is no living English author who has a stronger and deeper hold on the minds of the English community.'[3] In 1906 British Labour MPs were surveyed as to their favourite authors. Carlyle was the fourth most popular, only beaten by the critic John Ruskin, Dickens, and the Bible.[4]

It is Carlyle who gave us the phrase 'dismal science' to describe the study of economics. This throw-away quip about economics is still trotted out constantly in public debate. But it is, on investigation, incredibly revealing about the moral and ethical foundations of economics, the interconnection between open markets and an open society, and the egalitarian foundations of the liberal society.

The ethics of human equality at the heart of the democratic contract is also at the heart of laissez-faire economics. Those who seek to undermine the latter so often rest their claims on the former. In this chapter we will consider anti-free market thinking at its worst—through the romantic racism of Thomas Carlyle to the scientific racism of the eugenicists in the progressive economics movement. In the next chapter we narrow the opposition to human equality and free market economics to the paternalists of the twenty-first century—informed, as they are, by new doctrines of public health and anti-consumerism.

Carlyle was a romantic in the nineteenth century sense. He believed that the world which had been created by the industrial revolution was heartless and capitalistic. He imagined humans were divided into two opposed and mutually exclusive halves: the soul, which embraced mysticism, romance and the divine, and a selfish, calculating side which was individualistic and unsentimental. Carlyle worried about the 'mechanical age' with its machines and industry, and opposed laissez-faire economics and the 'God of Mammonism.' He once complained that 'political philosophy ... should tell us what is meant by "country", by what causes men are happy, moral, religious and the contrary. Instead, it tells us how flannel jackets are exchanged for pork hams'.[5]

Carlyle coined the 'dismal science' phrase in an essay titled 'An Occasional Discourse on the Negro question', published in *Fraser's Magazine* in 1849.[6] Apparently dissatisfied with the meekness of this title—a title the editors of the magazine may have insisted on—Carlyle republished the essay a few years later as 'Discourse on the Nigger Question'.

The essay was a full throated argument to reintroduce slavery in the West Indies, a stern polemic against the anti-slavery movement, and an aggressive defence of racial hierarchy. Carlyle's argument was as follows. The anti-slavery movement (known colloquially as 'Exeter Hall' after the London venue for meetings of the anti-slavery society) had allied with classical economists to agitate for abolition. Yet, having freed the slaves, they now ignored the natural experiment that abolition had provided them. In Carlyle's view, the now-free black population of the West Indies lived off the land growing pumpkins for themselves rather than working the sugar and cinnamon crops 'for the benefit of all mankind'. The economists said that labour would be regulated by the laws of supply and demand. But Carlyle believed that freed slaves were so lazy that the laws of supply and demand did not apply to them. The only way to mobilise the black labour force in the West Indies was through the 'beneficent whip'.

Carlyle believed that there was a natural hierarchy of races, which corresponded to their moral, intellectual, and cultural virtue. He had argued elsewhere that society was to be bound together by 'a mystic miraculous unfathomable Union'.[7] Within that union, the white races were at the top. The lesser races were below. Slavery, or at least servitude, was the natural order.

> That, you may depend on it, my obscure Black friends, is and was always the Law of the World, for you and for all men: To be servants, the more foolish of us to the more wise; and only sorrow, futility and disappointment will betide both, till both in some approximate degree get to conform to the same. Heaven's laws are not repealable by Earth, however Earth may try,—and it has been trying hard, in some directions, of late! I say, no well-being, and in the end no being at all, will be possible for you or us, if the law of Heaven is not complied with.[8]

Economics was 'dismal' because it had no room for the sort of moral judgements about the differing virtues of the races; because it admitted no room for distinguishing natural differences.

> Truly, my philanthropic friends, Exeter Hall Philanthropy is wonderful; and the Social Science—not a 'gay science,' but a rueful—which finds the secret of this universe in 'supply-and-demand,' and reduces the duty of human governors to that of letting men alone, is also wonderful. Not a 'gay science,' I should say, like some we have heard

of; no, a dreary, desolate, and indeed quite abject and distressing one; what we might call, by way of eminence, the dismal science. These two, Exeter Hall Philanthropy and the Dismal Science, led by any sacred cause of Black Emancipation, or the like, to fall in love and make a wedding of it,—will give birth to progenies and prodigies; dark extensive moon-calves, unnameable abortions, wide-coiled monstrosities, such as the world has not seen hitherto![9]

Carlyle's thought was fundamentally hierarchical. In his lectures *Heroes and Hero-Worship* he conceived of an order determined by authority figures who knew what the masses themselves desired better than the masses knew. At the top of the hierarchy were heroes of 'originality, sincerity, [and] genius'. As he wrote, 'The man of intellect as the top of affairs: this is the aim of all constitutions and revolutions, if they have any aim.'[10]

Thomas Carlyle is an extreme but revealing example of the relationship between hierarchy—in his case, including but not at all limited to racial hierarchy—and hostility to *laissez-faire* economics. Carlyle was not a socialist. He was a Tory opposed as much to the revolution of the state as the revolution of the market. The argument he presented in his 'Negro question' essay was significant: there are, in his view, a group of humans that are immune to the laws of supply and demand. Economic logic could not regulate the former slaves. The dismal science had failed in the West Indies. The only solution, for Carlyle, was to abandon 'perfect equality' and reintroduce slavery.

Carlyle's friend, John Stuart Mill, responded to the pro-slavery essay in the next issue of Fraser's Magazine. Mill wrote of West Indies slavery, 'I have yet to learn that anything more detestable than this has been done by human beings towards human beings in any part of the earth.'[11] More fundamentally to Carlyle's claims, Mill argued that against the 'vulgar error of imputing every difference which he finds among human beings to an original difference of nature.' After all, hadn't there been many great 'negro' civilisations? The greatness of Egypt inspired the Greeks. But even if that had not been the case, Mill made an ultimately moral argument:

> were the whites born ever so superior in intelligence to the blacks, and competent by nature to instruct and advise them, it would not be the less monstrous to assert that they had therefore a right either to subdue them by force, or circumvent them by superior skill, to throw upon them the toils and hardships of life, reserving for themselves, under the misapplied name of work, its agreeable excitements.[12]

In his magnum opus *Human Action*, the Austrian economist Ludwig von Mises describes views that people like Carlyle held as 'polylogism'—the idea that different groups of people reason differently.[13] The Nazis were the most famous polylogists: they believed that there was a specifically German logic and a specifically Jewish logic. Mises points out polylogism isn't limited to racialists. The Marxists believed that the human mind was determined by its social provenance. They rejected the idea of a universal logic or reasoning. Each social class had its own logical system determined by its material environment. Thus Marxists could talk about 'bourgeois' science, as if science conducted in a capitalist society was distinct to the science which would prevail in a non-capitalist economy. Mises' rejected polylogism to argue that, in fact, all humans were driven by the same basic principles: they acted purposefully to achieve their desired ends. As such, humans respond to incentives and interact with each other independently.

Yet the obvious undercurrent to all polylogist thought was

not just that some groups thought differently, but that some groups thought better. Those with superior reasoning ought to be given social power, and those with inferior reasoning ought to be placed on the lower ranks of a social hierarchy, if not eliminated from it.

What made the economists like Mill and Mises revolutionary was their insistence that all actors in the economic system be treated equivalently; that they be given the same weight in the social order. In Mill's utilitarianism thought, the goal was to produce the greatest happiness for the greatest number. It was not to produce the greatest happiness for a group. It was not to allocate happiness according to virtue or intelligence or ethnic purity. Rather, Mill assumes that all individuals have the same moral worth. All have the same potential to participate in the economic, social and political system.

David M. Levy and Sandra Peart call this approach 'analytical egalitarianism'.[14] It is a philosophical approach that unites Adam Smith and John Stuart Mill with modern social democratic philosophers like John Rawls. In Smith's view, the competitive market process opened social betterment to all people. Unlike the cartelised markets of his day, a free market offered opportunities to those without political power or hierarchical position. Centuries later, Rawls revived the tradition of analytical egalitarianism to conclude that 'fairness' required equal treatment.

Economic analysis is shaped more by moral reasoning than is commonly recognised. Its methods of reasoning require the imposition of ethical presumptions that govern how happiness—utility—is treated. The classical utilitarians profess to draw quasi-scientific principles on which legislation can be based but those principles cannot avoid implied moral claims.

Mill was particularly forthright about his belief that individual liberty had to be part of the quantum of happiness, arguing in his most read book *On Liberty* that while he regarded 'utility as the ultimate appeal on all ethical questions ... it must be utility in the largest sense, grounded on the permanent interests of a man as a progressive being.' Translating this into modern jargon, a calculation of welfare or well-being depends much on values of who is doing the calculating.

The English jurist Henry Maine told a story of meeting an Indian Brahmin and trying to to describe the theories of Mill and Bentham that individual happiness ought to be maximised. The Brahmin objected that this would not work: he was entitled to twenty times more happiness than the castes below him.[15] One could plausibly create an economic program where Brahmins' preferences are rated twenty times higher than the lower orders.

Treating individuals equally for the purposes of constructing a social order is not a claim that all people have equal capacities. It is not a scientific statement about the world. As we have shown in previous chapters, human society is characterised by a diversity of intellects and abilities. Rather, the claim for equal treatment is a moral claim. The economist Lionel Robbins wrote just before the Second World War that 'I do not believe, and I never have believed, that in fact men are necessarily equal or should always be judged as such. But I do believe that, in most cases, political calculations which do not treat them as if they were equal are morally revolting.'[16]

Yet Robbins did not speak for the entire economics profession. Levy and Peart point out that the decline of *laissez-faire* economics in the second half of the nineteenth century went hand in hand with the abandonment of the analytical egalitarianism that sustained it. The consequences were substantial. It is an uncomfortable truth that the economists in the progressive era who persuaded governments to regulate and control the economy also pursued and articulated racialist and paternalistic doctrines. The close connection between eugenics and progressive economics has not been well recognised. The same organisations that urged governments to introduce minimum wage laws, food and drug regulation, impose income taxes, trust-busting, and environmental regulation, also urged governments to restrict immigration on the grounds of race and remove the unfit and degenerate from the economic sphere.[17]

This interconnection reached the very top of the intellectual progressive tree. The English economist Arthur Cecil Pigou has come down in history as a pioneer of welfare economics—the field of study that concerned itself with market failures and the possibility of government mitigation of those failures. In his 1920 book *The Economics of Welfare*, Pigou outlined the criteria by which governments ought to deal with positive and negative externalities. These principles are still taught to economics students and constitute the basis of much economic reasoning in public policy debate. Yet Pigou's book is itself largely unread, so students and policymakers miss the eugenicist elements of his thought. Pigou advocated the segregation of 'tainted persons'—by reason of criminal activity or mental illness—from society, and even their sterilisation, to prevent their criminality or psychological deficiency from being propagated to future generations. In his view, 'such a policy would redound both to the general and to the economic welfare of the community'.[18]

In an earlier essay, published just before he was made Professor of Political Economy at the University of Cambridge (a post which made him the academic heir of the great economist Alfred Marshall) Pigou based his argument for social welfare policies on a biological footing. Stressing that environmental factors were a major contributor towards the propagation of poverty down the generations, he argued for government policy to alleviate those environmental problems. However, he observed that many poor communities had relatively high reproductive rates. Applying Darwinian principles to this observation suggested that the poor were selecting away from positive economic traits—that is, poverty was reproducing itself on a biological basis. While Pigou shied away from the full-blown eugenicist solution to this problem—he only advocated sterilisation of 'imbeciles, the idiotic [and] the sufferers from syphilis and tuberculosis'—he clearly saw welfare through a eugenicists' eye: as a biological hierarchy.[19]

Pigou was mild compared to some of his contemporaries. The history of the early American Economic Association is littered with eugenicists and racialists. In their first decades the *Quarterly Journal of Economics* and the *Journal of Political Economy* were full of articles about immigration and race. As an example—and a representative one at that—one of the American Economic Association's early publications was titled *Race Traits and Tendencies of the American Negro*. This tract argued that the high mortality of African-Americans was due to innate biological rather than environmental factors; a trait which was passed through the generation 'so long as immorality and vice are a habit of life in the vast majority of the colored population'.[20]

The progressive economists drew very clear policy lessons from their beliefs in racial hierarchies. The most obvious was immigration, an issue on which the eugenicists believed that policy makers had not paid enough attention to heredity. As one prominent economist, Prescott Hall, wrote in 1912, 'the instincts and habits which cause a low standard of living, willingness to underbid native labor, and migratory habits are maters of race and inheritance'.[21]

That great progressive achievement, the minimum wage, was another policy recommendation of the eugenicists. In the twenty-first century the debate over the minimum wage concerns whether it causes unemployment. The progressive economists were not sceptical about this question. They knew that by artificially raising the lowest wages some people would be kicked out of work. They saw this as beneficial, as those who would be made unemployed were racially inferior. Henry Rogers Seager, professor of political economy at Columbia University and a future president of the American Economic Association wrote, 'The operation of the minimum wage requirement would merely extend the definition of defectives to embrace all individuals, who even after having received special training, remain incapable of adequate self-support.'[22] Those who had been proven 'undesirable' by their inability to sell their labour at the minimum price would be dealt with by isolation or sterilisation. Another future president, A. B. Wolfe, argued that the minimum wage would remove from employment workers 'who are a burden on society'.[23] Woodrow Wilson's Commissioner of Labor, Royal Meeker, a Princeton professor of economics, argued that

> It is much better to enact a minimum-wage law even if it deprives these unfortunates of work … Better that the state should support the inefficient wholly and prevent the multiplication of the breed than subsidize incompetence and unthrift, enabling them to bring forth more of their kind.[24]

These are hardly marginal figures. Indeed, the eugenic

progressives were at the peak of their profession, and at the forefront of other battles for interventionist and regulatory controls over the economy. Henry Rogers Seager was one of the first American advocates of social security. Royal Meeker was a key figure in the Woodrow administration's program of expert-driven bureaucracy.

Why were eugenics and progressive economics so closely intertwined? As Thomas C. Leonard writes, the beliefs which informed the latter were strikingly similar to the beliefs that informed the former.

> Progressive opposition to *laissez faire* was motivated by a set of deep intellectual commitments regarding the relationship between social science, social scientific expertise and right governance. The progressives were committed to 1) the explanatory power of scientific (especially statistical) social inquiry to get at the root of social and economic problems; 2) the legitimacy of social control, which derives from a holist conception of society as prior to and greater than the sum of its constituent individuals; 3) the efficacy of social control via expert management of public administration; where 4) expertise is both sufficient and necessary for the task of wide administration.[25]

There remains the possibility that one could be a racialist—that is, could believe in innate racial characteristics, a hereditary hierarchy—and still be a supporter of *laissez-faire*. In other words, while believing that certain races were scientifically superior to other races, it would be possible to still believe that all races should be treated equally under the law. This is an important question: it goes to the heart of the relevance of analytical egalitarianism, and indeed, many of the issues in this book. If science demonstrated to analyst's satisfaction that there was a natural human hierarchy, would it be possible to nevertheless hold human equality up as a political philosophy? Levy and Peart quote Sidney Webb, one of the founders of the Fabian Society and the London School of Economics and a notable eugenicist, who said that

> The policy of '*Laisser faire*' is, necessarily, to a eugenicist the worst of all policies, because it implies the definite abandonment of intelligently purposeful selection … No consistent eugenicist can be a '*Laisser faire*' individualist unless he throws up the game in despair. He must interfere, interfere interfere![26]

It would be an unhappy eugenicist who was both convinced that the inferior races were outbreeding the superior ones and still believed that intervening in that process was wrong or would be ineffective. It is theoretically possible to believe that human difference is innate and morally significant and nevertheless reject that belief as a basis for political and economic organisation. But in practice of course the *laissez-faire* eugenicist was a rare, if non-existent, breed.

Nineteenth century critics of classical economics based their objection to the free market liberalism of writers like Adam Smith on precisely the heterogeneity of humanity. More often than not that heterogeneity was determined by race and national characteristics. Gustav Schmoller, the leader of the German historical school, claimed that 'In the eighteenth century the science of State, of society and political economy shared … the belief in the natural equality of men', as if there was a 'human nature in general'. Schmoller objected that 'there is no general character of man'. Rather, economists must base their analysis on the character is specific races and nationalities.[27] On this foundation Schmoller and his followers urged the German state to pursue social reform—such as fair wages and factory regulation—and reorientate trade policy towards national goals.

That Schmoller, Carlyle and the eugenicists based their opposition to market liberalism on their belief in fundamental human difference is significant. To use the machinery of the state to interfere—that is, control, regulate, direct—with the free choices of another person is to assume both the competence to do so and the moral legitimacy of doing so. The eugenicists, in particular, were the consummate experts of the day. We should not be blinded by our moral revulsion to their beliefs from recognising that they—and the society they lived in—saw their work as the epitome of scientific endeavour. They used the most advanced statistical techniques and, more than their predecessors, collected swathes of social science data to back up their claims. They believed that their scientific knowledge legitimised a program of social reform that prevented and redirected the biologically suboptimal choices of their subjects. In their view, their program was moral precisely because it was scientific.

As a consequence, they were under no illusions about the foundational moral beliefs of the market liberals who they opposed. The market economy, in their mind, was one based on a fallacious belief in human equality. The doctrine of non-interference was a rejection of human difference, of scientific expertise, and of natural hierarchy. It was wrong because it treated people as morally equal. The twentieth century free market economist William Niskanen described the ethical precepts of market liberalism in this fashion:

> The primary moral case for a free market economy is that most economic decisions require the consent of all those with the affected rights. No one has the authority to

dictate an outcome at the expense of another party, unless both parties have previously agreed to a contractual relation that grants this authority in specific cases. Freedom is an implicit moral value, because the concepts of good and evil have no moral meaning in the absence of choice. A free market economy, in summary, maximizes the conditions in which we are 'free to choose.'[28]

In the eugenicist or historicist view, however, free choice was exactly the problem. Not all races and societies were capable of exercising that free choice in an optimal fashion. Choices could be, to use a modern economics term, 'path dependent'— determined by the choices made previously. Races and nations could therefore transmit poor choices down throughout the generations. Only an elite of scientific experts could right them back on path.

CHAPTER
SEVEN

CONSUMERISM AND PATERNALISM

The history of ancient Athens has always been used as much as a metaphor as a description of a real civilisation in a real time and place. Study of the Athenian constitution and its history has been used to prove contemporary political points: to illustrate moral truths or to warn about the way states can fall into disrepair. This was never so true as during the revolutionary fervour of the enlightenment—an era when the greatest minds of the age were trying to envision a new political order based not on hereditary monarchy but on the rights of man. Athens, with its peculiar and distant democracy, was a yardstick by which all potential political systems were measured. Its birth and death were carefully studied to draw broader lessons.

For many enlightenment writers, Athens' decline was tied to its collapse into 'decadence'. The citizenry tended to seek out mere amusements and entertainment rather than what was in the interest of the state. One popular claim was that Athenians spent more money producing the plays of Sophocles and Euripides than they spent fighting the war against Persia.[1] To this, the best thinkers of the enlightenment tut-tutted: the Athenian state had directed all its attention towards producing luxury rather than maintaining its empire, and with fatal consequences.

This critique of democracy—that it favours indulgence over prudence—has its own ancient roots. In his *Republic*, Plato described a democratic figure as an analogy for the soul of democracy itself. This democrat followed its own desires, flitting about from obsession to obsession and reinventing himself according to whatever took his short-term fancy.

> Sometimes he drinks heavily while listening to the flute; at other times he drinks only water and is on a diet; sometimes he goes in for physical training; at other times, he's idle and neglects everything; and sometimes he even occupies himself with what he takes to be philosophy. He often engages in politics, leaping up from his seat and saying and doing whatever comes into his mind. If he happens to admire soldiers, he's carried in that direction, if money makers, in that one.[2]

As one scholar writes, Plato grants the democratic character no broad rationality and reasoning. The democrat is a 'rabble of desires, someone in whom order and unity have all but disintegrated.'[3] By his analogy between a democratic character and a democratic polity, Plato not only provided a critique of the two simultaneously but emphasised that the type of government an individual lived under shaped their character. A person living in a democracy had a different character to that living in a monarchy or tyranny. His democrat had been freed to live a life of its pleasing—to pursue its own desires. In Plato's assessment, that democratic life was insubstantial and disorderly.

Obviously this critique had much to do with the elitist foundation of Plato's political thought, and his belief that the ideal state was ruled by philosopher-kings. Yet his critique ought to be familiar to us. One of themes of twentieth and twenty-first century public debate is a moral claim that the modern political order permits or encourages individuals to indulge themselves on consumption or amusements that are, on some ethical or practical measure, unhealthy for them.

This modern critique differs from the critique presented by Plato in one superficially important way: it is targeted not at democracy but capitalism. In other words, indulgence is seen as a disease of the economic, rather than political system. In our contemporary debate that disease is more widely known as 'consumerism'. Plato's distaste for frivolous amusements has become a distaste for the acquisition of frivolous goods.

This is such a common complaint that it ought not to require too much elaboration. A survey of anti-consumerist rhetoric included complaints that under capitalist society people were 'preoccupied with materialist things ... the frivolous accumulation of goods for their own sake'.[4] Another argument is that this frivolous accumulation has crowded out higher virtues: 'modern consumerism seems to violate traditional American values about the work ethic, self-restraint and participation in voluntary associations ... [consumerism] eat[s] away at family time, neighbourhood cohesion and public solidarities'.[5] In a 1995 encyclical Pope John Paul II made such an argument within a religious frame:

The eclipse of the sense of God and of man inevitably leads to a practical materialism, which breeds individualism, utilitarianism and hedonism. Here too we see the permanent validity of the words of the Apostle: 'And since they did not see fit to acknowledge God, God gave them up to a base mind and to improper conduct' ... The values of being are replaced by those of having. The only goal which counts is the pursuit of one's own material well-being. The so-called 'quality of life' is interpreted primarily or exclusively as economic efficiency, inordinate consumerism, physical beauty and pleasure, to the neglect of the more profound dimensions-interpersonal, spiritual and religious-of existence.[6]

Just as the enlightenment writers believed that the Athenian taste for amusements was ultimately contrary to Athenian self-interest, modern critics of consumerism argue that consumers are ultimately harming themselves. The catchy word here is 'affluenza' which describes prosperity as a disease. The Australians Clive Hamilton and Richard Denniss define affluenza in three parts, scaling from individual psychological consequences to a broad social disorder:

1.) The bloated, sluggish and unfulfilled feeling that results from efforts to keep up with the Joneses. 2.) An epidemic of stress, overwork, waste and indebtedness caused by dogged pursuit of the Australian dream. 3.) An unsustainable addiction to economic growth.[7]

The analogy between society and the healthy or unhealthy body is notable. Society has an addiction. Stress, overwork, waste and indebtedness are an epidemic. The metaphor is seductive but incoherent (in what way is debt like an infectious disease?). Nevertheless, Hamilton and Denniss are playing on an ancient theme. Plato (through the dialogue he wrote as

Socrates) distinguished between two models of society. In the 'healthy city', citizens lived a life of austere satisfaction. They have modest desires which do not exceed the capacity for the city to provide. Their lives are happy, but their aspirations are limited.

> Will they not make bread and wine and garments and shoes? And they will build themselves houses and carry on their work in summer for the most part unclad and unshod and in winter clothed and shod sufficiently? And for their nourishment they will provide meal from their barley and flour from their wheat, and kneading and cooking these they will serve noble cakes and loaves on some arrangement of reeds or clean leaves, and, reclined on rustic beds strewn with bryony and myrtle, they will feast with their children, drinking of their wine thereto, garlanded and singing hymns to the gods in pleasant fellowship, not begetting offspring beyond their means lest they fall into poverty or war?

Not all are satisfied with life in the healthy city, however. Some citizens strive for more. In an alternative society—the 'luxurious city'—citizens desire more than just the necessities for a virtuous moral life. They seek comforts and extravagances.

> For there are some, it appears, who will not be contented with this sort of fare or with this way of life; but couches will have to be added thereto and tables and other furniture, yes, and relishes and myrrh and incense and girls and cakes—all sorts of all of them. And the requirements we first mentioned, houses and garments and shoes, will no longer be confined to necessities, but we must set painting to work and embroidery, and procure gold and ivory and similar adornments, must we not?'

These luxuries are, clearly to Plato's Socrates, both indulgently unnecessary and dangerous. The luxurious city, seeking to expand its prosperity beyond nature's limits, finds itself having to war and pillage in order to satisfy its desires. Plato's healthy city is, according to some writers, a proto-typical sustainable city—a model by which we can judge the contemporary world. For instance, two academic philosophers write that

> In our view, the most important things to note about the first city [the healthy city] are its modest size and its commitment to good and meaningful work aimed at producing what is needed. Its economy is based on mutual aid through the devoted production of necessities. The human-scale, locally-based economy of the healthy city isn't aimed at the endless acquisition of money, as the second city clearly is. Money and trade only serve to facilitate the sharing of goods that first brought the city into existence. In the second, luxurious city a population of wealthy consumers thrives, as well as a non-producing aristocracy. This city runs on the over-consumption and over-production of non-necessities as well as the misuse of natural resources, yet is unable to meet the basic needs of all of its citizens. The consumptive 'fever' of the luxurious city results in violence and the exploitation of its own citizens, as well as its neighbors.[8]

The intended comparison with contemporary politics is obvious. Plato believed that it was democracy which brought about harmful avarice, luxury and excess. Modern critics of affluenza and consumer capitalism believe that it is the market economy which brings about such vices. But these are ultimately the same complaint. The objection is directed at a social order which allows, or encourages, individuals to satisfy their own desires for luxury and consumption. In other words, it is the allowing of indulgences which is the problem. The anti-democrats and the anti-consumerists have different diagnosis of the root cause of greed and selfishness—democracy or capitalism—yet their concern is the same. People make the wrong choices, choices which harm themselves and society. The affluenza 'diagnosis' has people individuals working themselves sick for luxuries that they neither require nor gain any happiness benefit from.

Why would people act in such a counterproductive way, let alone an entire society? The answer offered today is that individual rationality is unable to withstand the onslaught of advertising, publicity, and the mass media in general. Advertisers—the vanguard of the capitalist class—manipulate basic human emotions such as love, desire, and envy in order to convince people to buy what they do not need. In this story, advertisers create the demand for consumption. As Hamilton writes,

> Today's consumer is not just sold products but persuaded over and over that spending money is an effective means to relieve them of their anxieties, self-doubt and the drudgery of their lives ...
>
> So when defenders of the market accuse critics of wanting to impose their views of appropriate consumption on others, what they are really doing is abandoning consumers to the overwhelming influence of the marketers.[9]

In his book, the *Price of Civilisation*, the economist Jeffrey Sachs spends a great deal of time describing what he sees as the pervasive and dangerous effects of 'technologies of mass persuasion', manipulating our consumer desires at a subconscious level. Sachs argued that 'unhealthy behaviors surely have reached a macroeconomic scale and raise deep questions about our well-being in an era of relentless advertising and excess.

Have we actually created a world that is programmed to undermine our very balance as individuals?'[10]

Once again, this is strikingly similar to the complaints made of Athenian democracy. Substitute the word 'demagogues'— the leaders of the *demos* who created and indulged desires for luxury and decadence—for 'advertisers' and the parallels are obvious. Sachs explicitly writes that the significance and scale of manipulation causes him to worry not only about its effect on individuals but on the population as a whole, hence his concern about the macroeconomic consequences of marketing. In his story, human beings are too psychologically weak to defend themselves against the predations of advertisers. Those who criticised the Athenian demagogues told the same story but without the veneer of sympathy for the masses.

The historian Moses Finley discussed three assumptions that underpinned ancient anti-demagogue writing. First, the population was unequal—morally, economically, socially, and (we could add) intellectually. Second, the population had a tendency to divide into factions according to its interests. Third, the ideal political order transcended these first two problems by overriding factional interest and directing the preferences of the masses towards the good life.[11] Sachs and others would no doubt reject that their worldview is supported by the first ancient assumption—that of moral inequality—as their diagnosis of the problem is founded on a general human frailty. Yet their solution is to substitute the revealed preferences of consumers with better preferences through taxation and regulation. Those substitutions have to be guided by expert knowledge. Thus, the hierarchical thought explored in Chapter 4 here is established.

One of the welcome things about Jacques Rancière's attack on anti-democratic thinking is that he ties together the distaste

of the populist masses with the modern distaste for 'narcissis-
tic consumerism' and individualism. Both harbour the barely
suppressed aristocratic disdain for the pastimes and pleasures
of the common people. As Rancière writes,

> [t]he denunciation of 'democratic individualism' works, at
> little cost, to coincide these two theses: the classic thesis of
> property-owners (the poor always want more) and the thesis
> of refined elites—there are too many individuals, too many
> people claiming the privileges of individuality. This is how
> the dominant intellectual discourse meets up with those
> censitaire [those who would restrict the franchise according
> to property requirements] and knowing elites of the nine-
> teenth century: individuality is a good thing for the elites;
> it becomes a disaster for civilization if everybody has access
> to it.[12]

With this frame in mind the hierarchical, aristocratic, and
fundamentally anti-democratic underpinnings of much contemporary debate is clear. State paternalism, whether from
the censorship of obscenities to attempted controls over what
we can eat and drink, is based on a dismissal and distaste for
Rancière's democratic excess.

Take obscenity regulation, for instance. The drive for censorship presumed a hierarchical relationship between censor
and the masses. The concern was always how obscenity and
blasphemy would affect and harm the population. More educated and elite readers and viewers were presumed to be immune from such depravations. It has always been the case that
censors are required to consume the content they censored—
their moral fortitude would protect them from damage. I have
mentioned in a previous work one ploy by a defence counsel in
an obscenity case in Melbourne in 1901, who cleverly asked an
academic witness for the prosecution whether the demoralising

effect he claimed a collection of French novels would have on the population would likewise effect, 'say, a Supreme Court judge'. The witness declined to answer, but the point was made.[13]

Obscenity and blasphemy are no longer the lynchpins of censorship, although neither have disappeared entirely.[14] Today the clearest manifestation over paternalistic hierarchy in modern public policy is the valorisation and empowerment of 'public health' experts to drive and direct regulatory controls over what the masses may and may not consume. The paternalistic foundations of public health regulation are the same as those which drive paternalistic censorship. It is no coincidence that one of the first uses of the phrase 'nanny state'— now the rhetorical *bête noire* of the public health movement— was deployed as a weapon against film censorship. In a 1960 issue of the *New Statesman*, the columnist William Whitebait wrote of the British Board of Film Censors, 'Novels and the Press get along, not too calamitously, without this Nanny; why shouldn't films?'[15]

The broad strokes of the case for public health paternalism is well-known, but it is worth briefly exploring the conceptual basis behind such interventions. We can divide them into empirical and ethical questions. In the former category, many arguments for public health regulation rest on the externality cost of individual behaviour. The most famous illustration here is second-hand smoke: the risk that an individual's choice to consume tobacco will negatively affect another individual who has not made that choice. Another common argument is the cost that smokers—or drinkers, or the obese—impose on our publicly provided health care system. These arguments are questions that can have empirical answers. Policymakers can ask how much health damage second-hand smoke causes to bystanders and how expensive taxpayer-funded medical care is relative to the excise tax imposed on the good in question.

Yet these empirical claims are typically mixed up with more fundamental claims about the ethics of allowing people to freely choose behaviour that might be seen as harmful or unhealthy. This is what we mean by paternalism—more formally, a situation where 'X acts to diminish Y's freedom, to the end that Y's good may be secured.'[16] In her strikingly-titled book, *Against Autonomy*, the philosopher Sarah Conly makes the argument for coercive paternalism, arguing that 'We need to limit people's freedom of action, their autonomy, in the interests of better living.'[17] Conly's book is an extended philosophical defence of the nanny state, offering a coherent and formal version of an argument that has been advanced by a large number of public health academics in specialist academic journals.

Conly bases her case on the degrees of human irrationality which we have discussed in this book. Cognitive biases prevent individuals from acting in their own enlightened self-interest. 'We generally suffer from many flaws in instrumental reasoning that interfere with our ability to make effective and efficient choices.'The solution, for Conly, is coercion:

> Coercive paternalism takes certain decisions out of our hands. It does this in order to help us do what we want to do, which is to lead longer and happier lives. We know that leaving people to fend for themselves is too often simply not successful in getting people where they want to go. Instead of letting people languish in the misery cause by their own decisions, why not intervene, as we do with prescription drugs, as we do with seat belts, and help people out?[18]

In building her case for coercive paternalism, Conly makes much of the fact that measures of 'soft' paternalism, such as information provision about the consequences of unhealthy or harmful behaviour, have failed to eliminate that unhealthy or harmful behaviour. But her evidence on stubborn irrationality is less strong than presented. For example, Conly points out that despite decades of anti-smoking messages and millions of dollars in public health advertising, 'more than 20 percent of the American population' does smoke.[19] In fact, updated figures from the Centre for Disease Control now show that figure is now 18.1 per cent, continuing a long term decline. This decline is consistent with spreading knowledge about the harms of smoking and therefore the much derided virtues of autonomy. She also claims that youth smoking has remained steady. This is also inaccurate. The sharpest decline in smoking rates between 2005 and 2012 were found in the 18-24 year old bracket—from 24.4 per cent in 2005 to 17.3 per cent in 2012. Nevertheless, even if Conly's assertions were correct, the stubbornness of youth smoking would not be inconsistent with human learning. Different generational cohorts have to learn anew the lessons of the previous generation. What matters is the persistence of behaviour over an individual's lifecycle—not how they behave before they have been subjected to a lifetimes' worth of learning.

By now it should be clear that the question we need to ask with paternalism, a political framework under which X diminishes Y's liberty in order to advance the good of Y, is: with what authority X does act? Conly is defensive on this point, arguing that coercive paternalism is legitimated by a functioning democracy: 'in a democracy, there needs to be general support for a program to continue'. Likewise, democratic institutions provide a protection, in her view, against aggressive paternalistic punishment and privacy violations. However, as we have seen, democracy is, as an instrumental principle of governance, a poor mechanism for controlling rulers.

Democratic legitimacy is not a binary question—it is not a question that has a simple yes or no answer. Rather, legitimacy, like democracy itself, exists on a continuum. Robert Dahl offers criteria (regular elections, freedom of expression, and so forth) by which we can judge *how* democratic a polity is, not *whether* it is democratic.[20] How legitimate coercive public policy is likewise depends on how effective the democratic system is at translating the desires of the political community into legislation. The worse it is at translation, the less justification there is for coercion. Coercion in democracy is harder to justify than it first seems.[21] The stronger the coercion, the higher the requirement that coercion be absolutely necessary for the good of the community, and the higher the requirement that the government is acting on behalf of the citizens, rather than against their will. Reaching those high requirements ought to require more than just the tenuous legitimacy provided by periodic elections.

This necessity for a high bar for coercion is all the more important when the coercion in question threatens the values which underpin the democratic community in the first place. Paternalism of the sort presented by Conly is specifically intended to constrain the autonomy of individuals within that community. But without the assumption of autonomy for citizens how can the democracy—needed, in her model, to protect against dangerous manifestations of paternalism—be justified?

Conly cites an argument advanced by Cass Sunstein and Richard H. Thaler in defence of the dispassionate planner. In their argument, planners are capable of making better decisions than those who are directly affected by the consequences of their decisions because they do not face the same direct temptations that might inspire the wrong choice. As Conly writes, the planner is 'able to make better decisions because he is not in those circumstances that prompt errors of judgment'.[22] This is a rather interesting reversion of principal-agent theory. In this story, agents are more capable of acting in the interests of principals because they can dispassionately assess what those interests are better than the principals.

It is a basic principle of accountability that individuals are more likely to act optimally when they personally bear more of the costs of their decision. This is the intuition behind attempts to mitigate principal-agent problems like employee share schemes and performance management. It is also a fundamental economic principle that underpins such phenomena as moral hazard (which describes the negative consequences of circumstances where individuals do not bear the cost of their own actions). Donald Boudreaux and Eric Crampton deploy this basic reasoning to argue that decisions are more likely to be optimal when individuals are both capable of choosing and have a personal stake in the consequences of that choice. All else being equal, we should expect that the 'rationality' of choices made by individuals is maximised when individuals bear the risks of those choices.

> [A] person has incentive to become adequately informed about impending choice situations only when that person is both decisive in, and personally impacted by, the decision. Stripping decisiveness or personal stakes from a decision maker moves him from the realm of rational ignorance, where there are real-world consequences attached to choices, to the realm of rational irrationality. Observed choices under such circumstances do not reveal the chooser's true preferences—i.e., the preferences the chooser would reveal if his choice were decisive.[23]

In context, however, Conly's principal-agent reversal makes sense, because ultimately her case for paternalism rests on the presumed utilitarian superiority of expert knowledge. 'Where such choices should be left to the chooser, and where intervention is permissible, will be a function of what is best described as a cost-benefit analysis, rather than a decision a priori that certain personal decisions should be sacrosanct.'[24] The folly of assuming that policy-makers can make such assessments—and can do so with the objectivity necessary for democratic legitimacy—is obvious.

Experts are as susceptible to the cognitive biases as anybody else. Indeed, as Boudreaux and Crampton argue, they are potentially more so. Without the disciplining force of bearing the consequences of their decisions, paternalists have more of an incentive to indulge the sorts of suboptimal behaviour that the human brain is vulnerable to. Hence the pervasiveness of expert overconfidence and groupthink.

There have been volumes upon volumes of papers and books written making the case for paternalistic intervention. Yet in this enormous body of work, there is an almost entirely absent recognition that cognitive biases effect both consumers and policymakers. One survey found that 95.5 per cent of academic papers in behavioural economics which proposed paternalistic policy action failed to take account of the cognitive ability of policymakers themselves. The study concluded that '[i]t does not seem satisfactory to simply assume that one set of actors is free from irrationality, without grounding this in psychological realism, while at the same time stressing such grounding as paramount for another set of actors.'[25] Back in the nineteenth century Jeremy Bentham pinpointed this disparately when he wrote that,

It is a standing topic of complaint, that a man knows too little of himself. Be it so: but is it so certain that the legislator must know more? It is plain, that of individuals the legislator can know nothing: concerning those points of conduct which depend upon the particular circumstances of each individual, it is plain, therefore, that he can determine nothing to advantage.[26]

It is hard not to see, in the public health critique, a philosophy similar to that espoused by the moral radical wing of the anti-consumer movement. Indeed, some have embraced this connection. Many paternalists have expanded their focus well beyond questions of information provision about unhealthy behaviours, and moved into the realm of cultural analysis.

Activists and bureaucrats now speak of a 'drinking culture', and give themselves the task of changing it. One Australian government public health document declares its intention to 'develop drinking cultures that support a reduction in alcohol-related harm'.[27] Public health academics have taken it on themselves to scrutinise popular music, film and television, searching out unhealthy messages that might be contrary to their political aims. This endeavour obsesses not just about seeing smoking in movies. Academic journals are full of papers purporting to expose the prevalence of drugs and alcohol in cultural expression. One study in 2013 looked at music videos shown on Australian television and concluded, terrifyingly, that 'references to alcohol generally associated it with fun and humour'.[28] Pressure from public health activists has led to museums airbrushing out images of cigarettes in wartime displays, even removing Winston Churchill's iconic cigar from his mouth.[29]

One might object that the nanny state and consumerist critique of modern society is not a hierarchical one: it does not presuppose that one group in society is superior to another, and therefore does not violate the principle of human equality which we have argued is the foundation of the democratic compact. Conly defends against such a charge by arguing that she supposes human cognitive error to exist on a continuum across the population, rather than dividing the population in to the capable and incapable. In her view, cognitive ability is dependent on circumstance, rather than innate ability.[30] Faced with the onslaught of advertising, psychological manipulation, and inherent temptation, all human beings are weak and unable to act in their own best interests. What is needed is not a class of superior beings, but merely a class of impartial spectators. In this argument, any individual thrown into power would be able to assess the evidence for paternalistic intervention and legitimately impose it upon others.

Yet this story has a gaping hole. We need to return to the question that opens this book: if we assume that people are not capable of choosing in their own best interest what they eat or drink, how they spend their money and how they arrange their affairs, then how can we assume that they are capable of participating in a democratic community? We have shown in earlier chapters that cognitive error and incentive misalignment is pervasive in the political arena, where the connection between choice—an individual's vote—and consequences—public policy decisions—are loose and uncertain. Why does the call for paternalism apply solely to consumers, rather than citizens?

The obvious answer is that, despite the valorisation of expertise, most public health activists and paternalists nevertheless, like Conly, see themselves as quintessential democrats. They see democracy as a blank slate for the legitimisation of coercive policy. As long as paternalism is subjected to the same processes as any other legislation—it is voted into law by a parliament that has itself been voted into power by citizens—it does not violate any fundamental political principles. Yet the cognitive dissonance of assuming that citizens are rational enough to vote but not rational enough to consume suggests that the philosophy of paternalism, if taken to its logical extent, is a political one, first and foremost.

CHAPTER
EIGHT

THE LIMITS OF DEMOCRACY

The worst tyranny of the twentieth century did not take power by force but through a vote. When in 1933 the Reichstag voted in support of an amendment to the German constitution that allowed Adolf Hitler's cabinet to make legislation without the approval of the Reichstag, Weimar democracy committed suicide.

Are there limits to legitimate democratic decision-making? The question raised by Nazi seizure of power is whether a democracy can act undemocratically—in that case, whether a democracy can vote itself out of existence. It was no secret that National Socialist German Workers' Party and Hitler were opposed to the entire Weimar structure. Nor was their intended repression of their political opponents at all hidden. The Nazi press had been publishing articles declaring their intentions to imprison opponents and German Jews in 'concentration camps'. Yet they commanded a large and increasing share of the vote.

There is a widely held but crude belief that any decision is 'democratic' as long as it has been subject to a vote, or merely represents popular opinion in some way. But constitutional constraints on democratic form are necessary to maintain democratic equality. Once again, we have to separate the outward manifestations of democracy—elections, polling booths, and campaigns—from the philosophy of human equality which underpins it. Then it is possible to construct rules, or at least principles, by which there can be a limit on what a democracy can do to itself and its citizens. The most obvious dilemma here is the existence of constitutional rules constraining democratic bodies. Are, for instance, bills of rights a violation of the democratic principle? It would have been better for history if Adolf Hitler's rise to power or his subsequent atrocities had been prevented by the Weimar Supreme Court (assuming for a moment that any such legal decision would not have been overturned by Nazi street force). But would it have been democratically legitimate? After all, Hitler had (an approximation of) a democratic mandate.

The last free election of Germany's Weimar Republic was held in November 1932. It was a disappointing election for the National Socialists—their 33 per cent of the vote was down on the previous high of 37 per cent recorded at a federal election just over three months earlier. 'We have suffered a set-back', wrote Joseph Goebbels privately.[1] Nevertheless, had been still a dramatic increase in support for the NSDAP in just a few years. In a May 1928 federal election the Nazi vote was just 2.6 per cent.

In January 1933 Adolf Hitler was appointed Chancellor of Germany by the elected President, Paul von Hindenburg, in part to prevent the threat of an army coup by the sitting conservative Chancellor Kurt von Schleicher. Now in power, although not yet with absolute power, the Nazis waged a campaign of terror against their opponents. The next election on 5 March 1933, was characterised by violence and intimidation. It delivered a substantial increase in support for the National Socialists. This election was dominated by the Reichstag fire, less than a week before polling day, which was blamed on the Communist Party. Hitler as Chancellor convinced Hindenberg to issue an emergency decree suspending all civil liberties— freedom of speech, freedom of public assembly, and so on—to counter the threat.

The March election still did not deliver an absolute majority for the Nazis. But these elections revealed the writing on the wall for Weimar. As Richard Evans points out, despite the failure of the Nazis to command a majority in November or March, 'What the elections did make clear, however, was that nearly two-thirds of the voters had lent their support to parties—the Nazis, the Nationalists, and the Communists—who were open enemies of Weimar democracy.'[2] The revolutionary Communist Party received just under 17 per cent support in November 1932. The far right German National People's Party found the support of another 8 per cent. Even the Catholic Centre Party—15 per cent support in November 1932—had almost entirely broken with Weimar democracy.

The measure that delivered Hitler final control over the German political system also came down to a vote in the Reichstag. Within 10 days Hitler brought the 'Enabling Act' to the Reichstag (which was now sitting in the Kroll Opera House under a swastika flag). The Enabling Act was a constitutional amendment which allowed the cabinet to govern and legislate without any reference to the legislature. The Enabling Act also permitted the government to deviate from the Weimar Constitution as it saw fit. While the law suggested that the Reichstag was to remain as a duly elected legislative body, the Enabling Act was the wholesale transfer of power from parliament to executive—in practice, of course, a transfer of power entirely into the hands of Adolf Hitler.

The vote in the Reichstag was not a free vote, but it was an indicative one. The 81 Communist Party deputies were banned from participating. Social Democrats were intimidated and a few were excluded. Even so, the Nazis could not command a majority vote on their own. The Enabling Act was passed with the support of the Centre Party and the Nationalists. Even the German State Party, the tiny rump of those that remained of the German liberal tradition of liberty and property rights, voted in favour of the bill. The final count was 444 to 94. Even if the Communists and all Social Democrats had been allowed to vote against the act, it still would have passed.

No recounting of the Nazi seizure of power should downplay the violence and thuggery that accompanied it, nor the constitutional weaknesses which allowed Hitler to gain power by emergency decree. However, it remains the case that Hitler's tyranny was voted into power. It was a dictatorship that had been elected.

The idea that a democracy is a small step away from a tyranny has been a longstanding objection to this political form. It could transition into a dictatorship, as it did in Weimar Germany, or it could become a 'tyranny of the majority'—a more subtle repressive state where the preferences of the majority outweigh and override the liberties of minority groups. Alexis de Tocqueville, the French traveller who visited the United States in the first half of the nineteenth century, is the most famous writer who worried about the tyranny of the majority, but in fact it has been a long theme throughout the debate over democracy. Athens' critics believed that a state where everything is up for a vote was not much different from an unconstitutional anarchy. Whichever faction could command a majority would have virtually dictatorial control over the state. This was a concern of Xenophon, Plato and Aristotle.[3] In his *Politics*, Aristotle wrote

> For tyranny is a kind of monarchy which has in view the interest of the monarch only; oligarchy has in view the interest of the wealthy; democracy, of the needy: none of them the common good of all.[4]

The framers of the constitution of the United States of America were deeply worried about the possibility that a majority could suppress, by lawful vote, the rights of the minority. John Adams was deeply pessimistic about the stability of democracy. He once wrote that 'Democracy never lasts long. It soon wastes, exhausts, and murders itself. There was never a democracy yet that did not commit suicide.'[5] For Adams one of the great fears was that in a government controlled by a single assembly the 'majority will instantly oppress the minority'.[6] Likewise, James Madison wrote in the Federalist Papers that in too many governments 'Measures are too often decided, not according to the rules of justice and the rights of the minor party, but by the superior force of an interested and overbearing majority.'[7]

The Weimar constitution's fatal flaw was its Article 48,

which allowed the president to pass emergency decrees without agreement of the Reichstag. By contrast, the American constitution features numerous constraints designed to prevent one arm of government dominating another, and to prevent the majority from trampling the rights of the minority. The separation of powers between the judiciary, legislature and executive is supposed to ensure no single body becomes dominant, and each provides a check upon the others. Each body is formed differently. The lower house of the legislature—the House of Representatives—is elected by popular vote. The president is elected by the electoral college. The judiciary is appointed by the executive. The upper house—the Senate—was also supposed to be loyal to the states. The Senate also provides a check on the populist lower house.

The Senate, in John Adams' view, was necessary to avoid having to rely on cruder and more inflexible mechanisms for preventing tyranny of the majority.[8] One example he had in mind was the *liberum veto* of the Polish-Lithuanian Commonwealth, one of the largest states in Europe that existed between the sixteenth and eighteenth century. The Polish state was an elected monarchy with a bicameral legislature, the *Sejm*. The upper house was an appointed collection of clergymen and upper nobility. The lower house was an assembly of noblemen, typically number in a few hundred. The *liberum veto* was a rule which required all votes in the *Sejm* to be unanimous. It gave each member a veto over legislation and, even, the capacity to end an entire session of parliament. This was a particularly powerful way to eliminate the tyranny of the majority problem by giving even the smallest minority an override if legislation was not seen in their interest.

It has, for a long time, been a standing belief that the *libe-*

LIBERTY, EQUALITY & DEMOCRACY

rum veto was one of the major factors which led to the downfall of the Polish state. The veto meant that any legislative decision could be blocked by a recalcitrant member of the *Sejm*. What was worse was that the Russian government was bribing members to nullify parliaments, weakening the state for its eventual partition and conquest at the end of the eighteenth century. One estimate suggests that of 55 sessions of the *Sejm* after 1652 only seven successfully passed legislation.[9] The lesson that enlightenment thinkers drew from this was that the Polish unanimity rule was one minority protection too far. John Adams wrote that 'One fool, or one knave … bribed by an intriguing ambassador of some foreign power, has prevented measures the most essential to the defence, safety, and existence of the nation.'[10] For Benjamin Constant, the *liberum veto* 'did not make all the citizens free, but rather subjected them all to one person'.[11] And for Jean-Jacques Rousseau, the rule was once 'the guarantor of public freedom; now it is only an instrument of oppression.'[12]

Yet despite the bad press, the *liberum veto* was a rather effective way to deal with a central problem for the Polish-Lithuanian Republic: that of religious and political division. The Commonwealth was a very mixed religious state. The largest group was Roman Catholic, but it only constituted just over half of the population. In an era of religious persecution and sectarian violence the stability of the Commonwealth depended on the ensuring that Poland did not divide on religious lines. A requirement that all legislative decisions be unanimous was one way of virtually guaranteeing this. The *Sejm* was simply unable to pass a divisive religious law. The unanimity requirement ensured that, for instance, the Inquisition did not come to Poland.

It is easy in retrospect to argue that the *liberum veto* meant that Poland was uniquely vulnerable to Russian influence at the end of the eighteenth century. As Dalibor Roháč points out, it is not obvious that it was: Russian intervention consisted of much more than bribing politicians to exercise their veto, and in many ways the unanimity rule meant that harmful measures could not be imposed.[13] A rule that prevents good laws from being passed also prevents bad laws from being passed. But more fundamentally, the Polish-Lithuanian Commonwealth functioned for more than two centuries with the *liberum veto* in place. This is a rather impressive record for a relatively liberal and tolerant state in the early modern period.

Both the unanimity rule of the Polish-Lithuanian Commonwealth and the divisions of power in the American constitution are mechanisms to mitigate the democratic problem that collective action can be imposed on members of the collective who do not approve. The American model imposes non-majoritarian oversight—particularly the Supreme Court—and competing majoritarian institutions—the President, the bicameral legislature, and the states—to both slow down and check the actions of one arm of government with another.

But the American system begs a question: are unelected bodies, such as a judiciary, capable of overriding the elected legislature compatible with the democratic ethos? Alexander Bickel influentially described this as the 'the counter-majoritarian difficulty'.[14] In many countries the courts are able to override decisions of the legislature. The American system is heavily reliant on the Supreme Court reviewing legislation to see whether it is compatible with the American bill of rights. But this review process is often described as 'legislating from the bench'. When it strikes down a law as unconstitutional, the Supreme Court effectively makes public policy decisions that are contrary to decisions of the democratically legitimate legislature.

Jeremy Waldron has made the case against judicial review by pointing out that a society which believes in and respects individual rights can still have substantial disagreement about what those rights are. The judiciary that strikes down legislation assumes a consensus on the details of rights where none exists. In his view, 'judicial review of legislation is inappropriate as a mode of final decisionmaking in a free and democratic society.'[15]

However, Waldron bases his argument on a series of assumptions, the key assumption being that democratic institutions are 'in reasonably good order'. While on his grounds Western liberal democracies meet his criteria of universal adult suffrage, free and regular elections and so on, Waldron suffers from a deeper, unstated assumption that these institutions are effective mechanisms for making collective choices. Ilya Somin has made the argument that deep political ignorance within the American electorate (a problem shared by the Australian electorate) makes deference to the legislature much less valid. As Somin argues,

> If most of the electorate has little or no information on politics and government policy, it is likely that legislative output does not represent the will of the majority in the way Bickel and later theorists assumed. Judicial invalidation of such legislation, though potentially problematic for any number of other reasons, is not nearly as 'countermajoritarian' as generally supposed.[16]

In other words, the criticism of judicial review is far less robust when we relax the assumption that majority decision making is efficient or when we take into account democratic principal-agent problems.

Majoritarian decisionmaking is not the only test of democratic legitimacy. If it were, the Nazi seizure of power would have been a 'democratic' one, and all democracies would be constantly teetering on the brink of tyranny. Likewise, at the other extreme, if majority rule was the singular test of democratic governance then the Athenian method of allocating administrative offices—by drawing lots, that is, sortition—would be democratically illegitimate. After all, the lucky winner of the random draw had not been voted in or approved by a majority of the demos.

One of the most common arguments made against bills of rights and judicial review is that they violate the sovereignty or supremacy of the legislature. This argument is less strong than it first appears. The original formulation of a bill of rights has to be instituted through a democratic system. In the case of some Australian states, bills of rights have been introduced as statutes by the parliament. These statutory bills of rights exist as speedbumps for the legislature, intended to require parliament to consider the effect that legislation may have on rights protection. Any constitutional bill of rights—one that would empower the judiciary to overrule legislation—would have to be introduced through a referendum; being granted its democratic legitimacy through that process. (Indeed, the introduction of a constitutional bill would be more democratic than a statutory one, which would require the voter themselves, rather than their agents, to approve of the new rules.)

But more critically, it is an acceptable principle of liberal government that each wing of government is constrained by some system of rules. Most liberal countries have a constitution that tightly limits what the legislature and executive can do; one that can only be modified by a higher standard of voter consensus than normal legislation. Such rules prevent democratic governments from becoming government by arbitrary rule. The existence of an elected leadership does not vest that leadership with an unlimited mandate. Public support, made manifest through the act of voting, sometimes encourages politicians to believe that they have the 'right' to rule, and that they have the authority to rule as they please. A well-written constitution imposes boundaries on their actions.

Similarly, if we accept that the mechanisms for democratic accountability are flawed, a constitution is necessary to restrict government action from becoming tyrannical. Benjamin Constant disposed of the supremacy of parliament or the executive argument in this compelling way:

> It does not follow, however, that the citizen body or those in whom it has vested the exercise of its sovereignty, can use it to dispose sovereignly of individual lives. On the contrary, there is a part of human existence which necessarily remains individual and independent, and by right beyond all political jurisdiction. Sovereignty exists only in a limited and relative way. The jurisdiction of this sovereignty stops where independent, individual existence begins. If society crosses this boundary, it becomes as guilty of tyranny as the despot whose only claim to office is the murderous sword. The legitimacy of government depends on its purpose as well as upon its source. When that government is extended to purposes outside its competence, it becomes illegitimate. Political society cannot exceed its jurisdiction without being usurpative, nor can the majority without becoming factious. The assent of the majority is not enough in all circumstances to render its actions lawful. There are acts which nothing can endow with that character. When a government of any sort puts a threatening hand on that part of individual life beyond its proper scope, it matters

little on what such authority claims to be based, whether it calls itself individual or nation. Even if it were the whole nation, except for the man it is harassing, it would be no more legitimate for that. If anyone thinks these maxims dangerous, let him think about the other, contrary dispensation which authorized the horrors of Robespierre and the oppressions of Caligula alike.[17]

So where can we draw the line on democracy? Democratically legitimate non-majoritarian institutions—laws, constitutions, rights, norms, and accountability mechanisms—are those designed specifically to mollify the possibility that a majoritarian vote might undermine the citizens' political equality. These can include the sorts of rights that are enumerated in a bill of rights—for instance, the right to freedom of speech, freedom of association and worship. Democratic theorists point to a bundle of characteristics that constitute a vibrant democracy such a free press. Legislation that undermines those characteristics, regardless of whether it was passed by a democratically elected legislature, undermines the democracy itself.

This reasoning does not provide any legitimacy for non-majoritarian institutions which are designed for some other purpose. For instance, non-majoritarian institutions which are intended to privilege experts with the goal of imposing their preferences on the majority do nothing to maintain democratic equality.

The obvious legitimate limits on democratic decision-making are those which reduce democratic accountability or the electoral system. We don't need examples as extreme as the Weimar republic to illustrate this point. In Australia's parliamentary system, legislatures have often tried to impose rules that would increase the competitiveness of the major parties relative to smaller, newer parties. These have variously been

changes to political party public funding, membership requirements for new parties, or donation laws which favour incumbent or established parties over new parties. Often dressed up
as attempts to 'level the playing field', these measures almost
always work for the benefit of the political parties that can
wield a majority vote in the legislature. It is not unusual to
see major parties offering such bills bipartisan support while
minor and micro-parties oppose. It would be hard to write a
rule that prevented such cartel-like behaviour—and possibly
dangerous to vest a non-majoritarian body such as the courts
with the responsibility for administering that rule—but the example should reinforce the fact that parliamentary supremacy
is hardly the only guiding democratic principle.

Political equality is more comprehensive than simply the
rights which allow free and fair elections or democratic discussion. Rather, political equality is a rejection of hierarchical
control—the imposition of the values of a higher order on a
lower order. These orders may be ranked by class or their heredity, or, as is more common in the developed world, by expertise.
Legislative action that undermines the basic moral equality at
the foundation of the democratic order is, in a very real way,
undemocratic.

CHAPTER

NINE

LEGITIMACY AND INEQUALITY

In his dialogue *Crito*, Plato recounts a conversation between Socrates and a wealthy Athenian named Crito. Socrates is in prison, having been convicted by an Athens jury of five hundred for bringing his own personal gods into the city—that is, not worshipping the gods of Athens—and corrupting the young. Socrates has broken the Athenian social contract. He has acted against the ethical and religious norms of the political community he lived in. The punishment is be execution.

Crito offers Socrates the chance to escape prison and certain death. It's a Socratic dialogue, so they have a debate. Socrates ultimately refuses Crito's help. Socrates argues that he has a duty to obey the laws of Athens. He owes everything to the city. Athens raised, educated and protected him. When he came to adulthood he did not reject the city's protection. Socrates therefore has an implied 'just agreement' with Athens, and has no right to reject it.

There is a longstanding debate about the contradiction between the attitude of Socrates at his trial (recounted in Plato's *Apology*) and the Socrates in *Crito*. At the trial Socrates appears as an individualist whose higher duty is to divine philosophy. To his friend Crito he presents himself as subordinate to the city. One explanation for this disconnect is that Plato wants to tell his readers that Socrates was a good citizen. Far from the deceitful and independent obscurantist that his accusers had presented him at the trial, the elderly philosopher was a modest and loyal Athenian. As George Grote writes, in Plato's telling

> Sokrates is thus made to express the feelings and repeat the language of a devoted democratical patriot … Hence it is all the better fitted for Plato's purpose of restoring Sokrates to harmony with his fellow citizens. It serves as his protestation of allegiance to Athens, in reply to the adverse impressions prevalent against him.[1]

There have been many attempts to resolve this contradiction, which, given the disconnect between Plato's Socrates and the historical Socrates, almost certainly reflect Plato's beliefs more than Socrates'. But in essence, the *Apology-Crito* contradiction is at the heart of our investigation into democracy. The question is how the moral autonomy of the individual can be reconciled with a coercive state whose legitimacy is founded on the free agreement of those individuals.

In the *Crito* Socrates presents a duty to obey, which ultimately results in the elderly philosopher giving up his life as a penalty for exercising his freedom of speech. His rights are subordinate to the state. Having signed the democratic contract, he must now accept its commands.

Of course the political and ethical context of Ancient Athens was different to ours—Athenian notions of free speech and political obligation were not the liberal individualist ones that most moderns share.[2] Nevertheless, the challenge raised in *Crito* is a very modern one. What resonates in Plato's work is not whether we have a duty to obey the state but whether it is just for the state—or the aggregated preferences of our fellow free citizens—to punish us for exercising our liberties. In essence, Socrates' crime was a crime of speech, but Athenians believed that he had acted to undermine the coherence of the political community. Athens prided itself on the fact that citizens were free to speak their minds. But that freedom only extended so far as the speech was democratically valuable. Socrates, who exposed the weaknesses in arguments through clever questioning and hypotheticals, was seen as manipulative and deceitful—the opposite of an honest democrat in the eyes of the Athenian jury which had convicted him.

As the Socrates case shows, a government that is founded on the basis that all the citizens are honest or good-natured will undermine the rights of those who are seen by their neighbours as dishonest or bad-natured. Nor ought government be founded on a claim that all citizens have equal intellectual ability, or even have equal interest in participating in the political system. These assumptions do not hold.

Likewise a democracy whose legitimacy rests on the informed participation of the citizenry will be a weak democracy. Modern government is impossibly complex. There is no way any citizen, no matter how dedicated to civic life, would be able to understand to any semi-informed level even a fraction of the policies which are presented in a typical election. Asking voters to understand the policies which are presented, legislated and driven between elections is even more fraught. Thousands of pages of legislation are passed every year. It would take an individual at least four dedicated weeks to read all the legislation before federal parliament at any given time, reading at an average reading speed, eight hours a day, five days a week.[3]

It is commonly observed that federal parliamentarians are ignorant of the basic elements of the legislation they vote on. This has become such a problem in the United States that some representatives have introduced a Read the Bills Act, which would require politicians to sign affidavits that they have read a bill before voting on it, and requires that bills are posted online long before scheduled vote.[4] And understanding legislation is not the same as merely reading it. Much new legislation amends existing legislation, or alters complex existent regulatory frameworks, whose consequences are only known to specialists. Parliamentarians are, in the principal-agent model of representative democracy, supposed to be the voters' delegates in the legislative world, but they often fail to play that role.

With such a high information costs for understanding government action, the idea that we could base democratic legitimacy on informed participation is the stuff of fantasy. Of course we need not demand absolute or even high levels of knowledge to consider voters informed. But the fact that parliamentarians—those whose job it is to read and understand legislation on our behalf—find it impossible to do so, gives strong reason to believe that the 'informed citizen' is a chimera, at least from the perspective of democratic legitimacy.

That information asymmetry between legislative drafters and voters also makes artificial attempts to create the informed citizenry somewhat farcical. The more informed a person is the more likely they are to vote.[5] Defenders of Australia's compulsory voting system often argue that compulsory voting compels greater engagement—that is, it creates an incentive for voters to seek out knowledge in order to make the bare minimum of a choice at the ballot box. Some studies have found that compulsory voting increases news intake and interest in politics.[6] But the fact remains that even those who claim to be interested in politics have seriously deficient knowledge and understanding of basic political facts and public policy issues—as we showed in Chapter 3.

The legitimacy of democracy has to be founded on something else. The case we have made in this book is that democracy has, as its moral foundation, the presumption of political equality—all individuals are morally equivalent. Democracy is the creation of a political community and legal framework based on the belief that (in the words of the Levellers' critics), 'every Jack shall vie with a gentleman and every gentleman be made a Jack'. There is no fundamental or natural hierarchy that places one individual or class above another.

It is human nature to create hierarchies. Ingroup bias gives force to human difference, creating blocs determined by shared characteristics, whether those are based on geographical location, cultural similarities or ethnic identity. Entire civilisations have been created around such hierarchical assumptions. Ancient Athens, for all its democratic virtue, was a slave society; slaves outnumbered free citizens. Aristotle believed in 'natural slavery', where it was just to enslave those who lacked autonomous rationality.[7] Feudalism divided society into hierarchical tiers of lordship and vassalage, creating a political order founded on that social inequality. The nobility had the right to participate in national politics where serfs did not. Nationalism divided human society into quasi-ethnic groupings—a hierarchy which was given its most extreme and genocidal form by the Nazi völkisch movement. This sort of explicit racist nationalism lives on in pariah states like North Korea, but a milder form is present when love of homeland becomes opposition to those outside the homeland. More common today are hierarchies based on religious difference, such as those violently manifest in the Middle East.

Thus democracy is an incredibly radical doctrine. It says that the only legitimate form of government is one which is constructed through the agreement of all people who live under that government. It rejects any basis on which a political hierarchy may be built—ethnic, racial, religious, nobility. A person's right to participate in the political community does not vary according to wealth or background.

Liberal theorists have called this principle equality before the law. For our purposes it might be better to describe it as equality before the state. This rephrasing captures the importance of the principle to democratic legitimacy, recasting it not as a relationship between the legislation and the individual but as the relationship between legislator and the individual. This avoids the unnecessary abstraction of 'the law'—legislation is human made. Legislation does not suddenly emerge out of the ether, it is written by bureaucrats acting on behalf of politicians who are themselves acting on behalf of constituents.

There is an obvious and critical objection to our argument in defence of moral equality. Does material inequality—the inequality of wealth that characterises any free society—undermine the democratic principles which we have valorised in this book? Anatole France, the French journalist and poet, mocked legal egalitarianism with his famous line 'In its majestic equality, the law forbids rich and poor alike to sleep under bridges, beg in the streets, and steal loaves of bread'.[8] The rule of law can be oppressive for those who lose out. Equality before the law provides little comfort for those who are oppressed by non-state forces—whether that is poverty, or social norms like racism and sexism. Those who love liberty should not dismiss the significance of these oppressive forces on human dignity and flourishing merely because they emanate from outside the state.

The challenge is even greater for us here because the doctrine of human moral equality is much more expansive than just equality before the law. It is based on the idea that there are no justifiable hierarchies on which to build a political community. Yet the political class represents only a narrow sliver of the population. Particularly in the United States, politics is dominated by those at the top end of the income scale. Likewise, people with wealth are freer to participate in the political community, whether with their time and energy, or by simply contributing money towards causes and political parties they support. In his blockbuster book *Capital in the Twenty-First Century*, Thomas Piketty imagines a resurgence of political hierarchy based on growing inequality, as a wealthy inherited elite are able to embed themselves in the political system thanks to their superior resources.[9] According to this argument, it is possible to maintain the formal structures of democratic equality—voting, freedom of expression, and so forth—yet have those preside over what is in effect a recreation of the hierarchical politics of the past.

This is a serious challenge. How can we meet it?

The framework presented here provides a guide. One the face of it, nothing in this book precludes some form of redistributive politics. Readers looking for a theoretical broadside against, for instance, progressive taxation or the welfare state ought to look elsewhere. There are of course many reasons to favour liberal, small government policies but we shouldn't imagine that democracy precludes alternatives.

Nevertheless, the relationship between liberalism and democracy is tighter than most people recognise. What any policy intervention must avoid is undermining the democratic precepts we have outlined. The key to evaluating redistributive policies is identifying the purpose behind the redistribution. Is it to provide a material safety net—that is, to prevent the sort of oppressive poverty that Anatole France describes—or is it to shift the balance of political power, as in the Piketty story? On the face of it, shifting political power away from those with material power might protect and entrench political equality. But the question isn't whether the goal is desirable—and obviously it is—but whether a democratic government can pursue that goal legitimately.

There are, as we have argued in Chapter 8, obvious and necessary restraints on the freedom of democracies to act. A parliamentary vote to end elections is obviously not democratically legitimate. Likewise, a parliamentary vote to punish political speech would undermine the foundation of the democracy itself, as the High Court's right to political communication cases has found. So can a democratic government seek to restructure political power—to shift the balance between the citizens whose moral equality provide it with legitimacy? If we accept along with Hayek that not all people are factually equal—there are vast differences not just in material wealth but in intellectual capability, political interest and so forth—then we open up an infinite range for possible 'redistributions'. But those redistributions will reintroduce exactly the sort of hierarchies that democracy is designed to remove.

Our argument here is that democratic government ought to be studiously neutral about the power relations between those who sustain it. This is not because material wealth and practical inequality is unimportant. Rather, it is because the founding principles of democracy presuppose such neutrality.

There have been many institutional changes proposed to prevent the emergence of political power founded on material wealth. One of the most direct ways wealthy people seek to influence government is through donations to political parties. It is no surprise then that political donations have been the epicentre of much policy attempt to restructure political power. As the former New South Wales Premier Kristina Keneally said when announcing restrictions on election funding and donation disclosure in 2010, 'those with the most money have the loudest voice and can simply drown out the voices of all others'.[10] According to this argument, placing bans and caps on donations would create a 'level playing field'.

Yet actively trying to manipulate the free debate and interrelations that underpin democratic legitimacy violates the principles we have outlined here. Nevertheless, the political donations issue gives us a hint of how to tackle the underlying problem. Money is attracted to the political system because the financial returns to political influence are so great. The question, as Gordon Tullock once asked, was not why there is so much lobbying, but, given the enormous windfall gains that lobbying can achieve, why there is so little.[11] (One possible explanation is that political donations and lobbying are not, as many people believe, a form of vote buying, but are rather a form of participation and consumption.[12])

This reasoning suggests why the principles of democracy, in our view, favours modest, rather than expansive government. Reducing the range of issues on which corruption can be targeted is likely to be more fruitful than trying to crackdown on the mechanisms of corruption. There's a reason that in Australia political corruption in recent years has centred around property development and mining licenses—it is in those areas where politicians have large amounts of discretion to make decisions with enormous financial consequence. To tackle corruption and perceptions of corruption the New South Wales government has banned political donations from property developers. But it kept the power to make development decisions. As successive scandals have demonstrated, even in the face of outright bans, money will flow in through backchannels as the rewards for influence are so great.

Reducing the disproportionate influence of wealth on a political system will require the reducing the power of the state—making that influence less desirable, rather than trying to cut it off with tightly written legislation. In other words, material inequality has political and democratic consequences, but those consequences are a function of the scope of government power, rather than the shape of the underlying inequality.

Thus we can answer Anatole France's challenge. No liberal society should tolerate such poverty that it causes homelessness. Much of the homelessness we see in contemporary society is the fault of deliberate policy decisions whose unintended consequences have raised the price of accommodation above the social safety net. In France's time he might have blamed the inadequate safety net. Either way, equality before the law is no assistance to those who are suffering in such a way, and equality before the law blind to the consequence of that law can be oppressive. Equality before the law is not the only principle on which policy ought to be designed. But neither is it a principle which can be discarded or degraded in pursuit of other goals. It provides the legitimacy by which policy decisions can be made. Equality before the law and policies designed to alleviate material deprivation are not mutually exclusive, but without the former the latter has no democratic authority.

The debate over the relationship between material equality and political equality is really a debate about the normative and positive approach of democracy. Political equality, so the argument goes, is a lovely ideal—like Gandhi's 'western civilisation'—but to describe actually existing democracy is in fact to describe massive inequalities: inequalities of power, inequalities of wealth, inequalities of interest and intellect. But we can cross the bridge between a description of the world as it is and a description of the world as we want it to be. Friedrich Hayek cautioned that that 'Nothing ... is more damaging to the demand for equal treatment than to base it on so obviously untrue an assumption as that of the factual equality of all men.'[13]

Yet equality does not have to be supposed or presumed. It is a reality. Equality is not a theoretical construct or philosophical gambit—it is a truth. This can be seen from observation of the world as it is. All rulers understand their vulnerability to replacement; all elite cultures see the cultures below themselves as a threat. As Jacque Rancière argues,

> Equality is not a fiction. All superiors experience this as the most commonplace of realities. There is no master who does not sit back and risk letting his slave run away, no man who is not capable of killing another, no force that is imposed

without having to justify itself, and hence without having to recognize the irreducibility of equality needed for inequality to function. From the moment obedience has to refer to a principle of legitimacy, from the moment is necessary for there to be laws that are enforced qua laws and institutions embodying the common of the community, commanding must presuppose the equality of the one who commands and the one who is commanded. Those who think they are clever and realist can always say that equality is only the fanciful dream of fools and tender souls. But unfortunately for them it is a reality that is constantly and everywhere attested to. There is no service that is carried out, no authority that is established with the master having, however little, to speak 'equal to equal' with the one he commands or instructs. Inegalitarian society can only function thanks to a multitude of egalitarian relations.[14]

There is nothing scarier to a believer in hierarchy that the fear that it might be supplanted.

CONCLUSION

Democracy is one of those abstract concepts, like liberty and equality and fairness, onto which philosophers and the public may impose wildly varying interpretations. This book has explored and defended one particular interpretation, founded in an underlying principle of human moral equality. The principle that each person is entitled to one vote equivalent with all others in society is a surprisingly deep one. To reject, as this principle does, the myriad of hierarchical relationships that civilisations have created over human history, is to make a series of philosophical claims about equality, capacity, and value with far-reaching consequences.

This interpretation takes democracy seriously, as a philosophical project in its own right. It is not, however, the only basis on which democracy is sometimes popularly justified. Many thinkers view democracy as simply a mechanism for facilitating the transfer of power between leaders without resorting to violence, and providing a safety-valve against the predations of the state. Friedrich Hayek summed up this position when he wrote in the *Road to Serfdom* that 'democracy is essentially a means, a utilitarian device for safeguarding internal peace and individual freedom. As such it is by no means infallible or certain.'[1] That is, democracy has an instrumental value insofar as it achieves the purposes we desire from it. It has no independent moral value; it is not valuable for its own sake. A further implication of this argument is that it would not reject the establishment of a political system which more effectively achieves the nominated goals—of protection of liberty and the stable transfer of political power. The instrumentalist might view Churchill's 'democracy is the worst form of government except for all the others' as a challenge—is there an even less worse form which we might adopt in the future?

Of course, actually-existing democratic systems do not in any way approach perfection. This book has looked at a number of institutional variations that are just as or even more 'democratic' than what we have today—particularly the Athenian system where government office was allocated by random change (sortition) or the Polish-Lithuanian voting system where any one member of the legislature could veto a proposal (the *liberum veto*). The criticism of both sortition and the *liberum veto* has been that they would result in suboptimal outcomes, the former bringing unqualified and incompetent people into the institutions of government and the latter allowing the decisions of the majority to be overridden by the tiniest minority. Discussions of democratic reform ought always to be alive to the practical consequences of any given system, as any institutional arrangement can have unintended consequences. But on the purely practical level, the problems with sortition and the liberum veto have been badly overstated. And the modern revulsion about these two mechanisms are indicative of a broader dissatisfaction—or even hostility—to the democratic principles which underpin them.

Any basis for political order is necessarily founded on assumptions about who legitimately rules and the limits to their power. These questions are not essentially utilitarian. They have moral content. Government is itself inevitably hierarchical. Through this frame we can see that the democratic movement has been much more than just the establishment of, for instance, the House of Commons or the expansion of the franchise, but has been to reduce and where possible eliminate as much of the hierarchical structure of government. The rule of law sought to eliminate the legal privileges of power by applying law to the ruler and the ruled equally. The replacement of monarchical power with parliamentary power has given those who do not have birthright or title an opportunity to participate in the operation of government.

That is, democracy is anti-elite. William F. Buckley famously said that he would 'sooner live in a society governed by the first two thousand names in the Boston telephone directory than in a society governed by the two thousand faculty members of Harvard University'. His was not a disdain for intellectualism but for the fantasies of the intellectual establishment—those at the top of the intellectual hierarchy. Buckley made this statement at a time when the Kennedy administration had adopted the pretence of technocratic rationalism as a form of government. Public policy problems—even questions of war and peace—could be resolved through the brute force of intellect. Robert McNamara, John F. Kennedy's Secretary of

Defence, claimed that 'the real threat to democracy comes, not from over-management but under-management'.[2] McNamara was one of the whiz-kids, the academics and intellectuals that Kennedy brought into government to implement government by 'rational decision making'. The fact that their expertise was not necessarily in the areas they were asked to oversee was not germane. McNamara was an incredibly intelligent former manager of the Ford Motor Company but he 'knew nothing about Asia, about poverty, about people, about American domestic politics, but he knew a great deal about production technology and about exercising bureaucratic power'.[3] The problem is not the existence of elitism or human difference, it is the translation of the empirical observation of human difference into a philosophy of government.

Buckley's line, therefore, is not just a side-swipe at the elite intellectuals of his day, but a defence of human equality. In his book *The Lucky Culture*, Nick Cater powerfully argues that a 'self-appointed ruling class of sophisticates' has captured Australian public debate, with detrimental consequences for the egalitarian Australian national character.[4] This anti-elitist argument of Buckley and Cater has an old and storied history. John Locke had much the same feelings. Jeremy Waldron, in his study of Locke's thought, characterises the 'democratic intellect' as a theme throughout Locke's writing, disparaging the pretences of the intellectual classes. Locke ridicules the 'all-knowing Doctors', 'learned disputants', 'Flatterers who talk to amuze Peoples Understandings', the 'learned gibberish' of the intellectual classes with their 'multiplied curious Distinctions, and acute Niceties', the intellectuals who

> cover their Ignorance, with a curious and inexplicable Web
> of perplexed Words, and procure to themselves the admira-

tion of others, by unintelligible Terms, the apter to produce wonder, because they could not be understood.[5]

The philosophy of democracy is at once both intuitive and radical. Intuitive because egalitarianism is at the heart of many of our popular ideals—there are few in the modern world who would dispute the rightness of one person, one vote. Yet it is radical because it implies far more consequences than simply the construction of a voting system or political order. Human moral equality is a rejection of hierarchy—the hierarchy that manifests itself in such diverse ways as monarchy, the racial pyramid, paternalism, the cult of expertise, and anti-consumerism.

At the final reckoning, democracy is terrifying because it is of the radical notion that nobody—nobody, no matter how rich, no matter how noble, no matter how virtuous, no matter how intelligent or expert—is superior. Nobody has the 'right' to rule.

REFERENCES

Introduction

1. A. S. P. Woodhouse, *Puritanism and Liberty: being the Army Debates (1647-9) from the Clarke manuscripts with supplementary documents*, 2nd ed. (London: Dent, 1974), 53.

2. Cited in David Wootton, 'The Levellers,' in *Democracy: the Unfinished Journey, 508 BC to AD 1993*, ed. John Dunn (Oxford; New York: Oxford University Press, 1992).

3. Philip Baker, *The Levellers: The Putney Debates* (London: Verso Books, 2007).

4. A. S. P. Woodhouse, *Puritanism and Liberty: being the Army Debates (1647-9) from the Clarke manuscripts with supplementary documents*, 2nd ed. (London: Dent, 1974), 443-44.

5. Ibid., 52.

6. Ibid., 53.

7. Fergus Hanson, *Lowy Institute Poll 2012* (Lowy Institute for International Policy, 2012).

8. Alex Oliver, *Lowy Institute Poll 2014* (Lowy Institute for International Policy, 2014).

9. Griffith University and Newspoll, *Australian Constitutional Values Survey 2014* (2014).

10. Phillip Hudson, 'Dysfunction strips faith in politics,' *The Australian*, 10 October 2014.

11. Ian McAllister, *ANU-SRC Poll: Changing views of governance: Results from the ANUpoll, 2008 and 2014* (ANU College of Arts and Social Sciences 2014).

12. There is some dispute about whether the Greens should be considered a major party. See Guy Rundle, 'Greens a major party now?,' *Crikey*, 10 April 2014. The Greens regularly receive around ten per cent of the vote. This compares favourably to, for instance, the National Party. And as I've argued elsewhere, the Greens have 'been around for two decades and deserve to be treated as part of the mainstream.' Chris Berg, 'Micro-parties tap into dissatisfaction,' *The Drum*, 10 April 2014.

13. Margot O'Neill, 'Voters should have more say in policy,' *Lateline* (Australian Broadcasting Corporation2014).

14. Murray Goot, 'Distrustful, disenchanted and disengaged? Polled opinion on politics, politicians and the parties: an historical perspective,' *Parliament and Public Opinion*, Papers on Parliament 38 (2002).

15. Jackie Dickenson, "God Give Us Men': Attitudes towards parliamentary representation in Australia 1929–33,' *History Australia* 8, no. 2 (2013).

16. The University of Melbourne, Centre for Advancing Journalism,

and Our Say, *Citizens' Agenda: National Survey of Voters: Detailed Results* (2013).

17. James Bryce Bryce, *Modern Democracies*. (London: Macmillan, 1921).

18. Tim Soutphommasane, 'When wealth becomes king, democracy is a poor subject,' *Sydney Morning Herald*, 18 June 2012.

19. C. B. Macpherson, *The Political Theory of Possessive Individualism: Hobbes to Locke*, (Oxford: Oxford University Press, 2011).

20. Michael Mendle, ed. *The Putney debates of 1647: the army, the Levellers, and the English state* (Cambridge, U.K.; New York: Cambridge University Press, 2001); Wootton, 'The Levellers.'

21. Woodhouse, *Puritanism and Liberty: being the Army Debates (1647-9) from the Clarke manuscripts with supplementary documents.*

22. William Walwyn, 'W Walwins Conceptions; For a Free Trade,' in *The Writings of William Walwyn*, ed. Jack R. McMichael and Barbara Taft (Athens and London: University of Georgia Press, 1989).

23. Wootton, 'The Levellers.'

24. In this John Locke is an obvious and unfortunate culprit: see below and Jeremy Waldron, *God, Locke, and Equality: Christian foundations of John Locke's political thought* (Cambridge; New York: Cambridge University Press, 2002).

25. Hans-Hermann Hoppe, 'Demokratie. Der Gott, Der Keiner Ist,' http://archive.lewrockwell.com/hoppe/hoppe9.html.

Chapter 1

1. Ronald J. Hill, 'The CPSU in a Soviet Election Campaign,' *Soviet Studies* 28, no. 4 (1976).

2. Rasma Karklins, 'Soviet Elections Revisited: Voter Abstention in Noncompetitive Voting,' *American Political Science Review* 80, no. 2 (1986).

3. Howard R. Swearer, 'The Functions of Soviet Local Elections,' *Midwest Journal of Political Science* 5, no. 2 (1961).
4. Cited in ibid.
5. Many thanks to Charles Richardson for this information.
6. John Keane, *The Life and Death of Democracy*, (New York: W.W. Norton & Co., 2009).
7. Robert A. Dahl, *Democracy and its Critics* (New Haven: Yale University Press, 1989). p52
8. John Locke, *Two Treatises of Government* (Cambridge: Cambridge University Press, 1960).
9. Ibid.
10. King James Version, Genesis 9:16
11. David Hume, 'Of the Original Contract,' in *Essays: Moral, Political and Literary* (Indianapolis: Liberty Fund, 1987).
12. Adam Smith and Ronald L. Meek, *Lectures on Jurisprudence* (Indianapolis: Liberty Classics, 1982). p402-3
13. Carole Pateman, *The Sexual Contract* (Cambridge: Polity, 1988); Charles W. Mills, *The Racial Contract* (Ithaca: Cornell University Press, 1997).
14. Mills, *The Racial Contract*, 31.
15. Pateman, *The Sexual Contract*, 2.
16. James M. Buchanan and Gordon Tullock, *The Calculus of Consent: logical foundations of constitutional democracy*, (Indianapolis: Liberty Fund, 1999), 319.
17. Cited in Harro Höpfl and Martyn P. Thompson, 'The History of Contract as a Motif in Political Thought,' *The American Historical Review* 84, no. 4 (1979).
18. Woodhouse, *Puritanism and Liberty: being the Army Debates (1647-9) from the Clarke manuscripts with supplementary documents*, 356.
19. William Sharp McKechnie, *Magna Carta: A Commentary on*

the Great Charter of King John, with an Historical Introduction (Glasgow: Maclehose, 1914).

Chapter 2

1. Bruce Bueno de Mesquita and Alastair Smith, *The Dictator's Handbook: why bad behavior is almost always good politics*, 1st ed. (New York: PublicAffairs, 2011).
2. Cornelius Tacitus and Anthony Richard Birley, *Agricola and Germany*, Oxford world's classics (Oxford; New York: Oxford University Press, 1999).
3. Bruce L. Benson, 'The Evolution of Law,' in *The Encyclopedia of Public Choice*, ed. Charles Kershaw Rowley and Friedrich Schneider (Dordrecht; Boston: Kluwer Academic Publishers, 2004).
4. Henry Sumner Maine, *Lectures on the early history of institutions*, 7th ed. (S.l.: J. Murray, 1914).
5. Roger D. Congleton, *Perfecting Parliament: constitutional reform, liberalism, and the rise of Western democracy* (Cambridge; New York: Cambridge University Press, 2011).
6. F. Liebermann, *The national assembly in the Anglo-Saxon period* (Halle a. S.: M. Niemeyer, 1913).
7. J.C. Holt, 'The Prehistory of Parliament,' in *The English Parliament in the Middle Ages*, ed. R. G. Davies and Jeffrey Howard Denton (Manchester: Manchester University Press, 1981).
8. P. R. Cavill, *The English parliaments of Henry VII, 1485-1504*, Oxford historical monographs (Oxford; New York: Oxford University Press, 2009).
9. Albert Venn Dicey, *The Privy Council: the Arnold prize essay*, 1860 (London and New York,: Macmillan and co., 1887).
10. McKechnie, *Magna Carta: A Commentary on the Great Charter of*

King John, with an Historical Introduction.

11. Avner Greif, 'Commitment, Coercion and Markets: The Nature and Dynamics of Institutions Supporting Exchange,' in *Handbook of New Institutional Economics*, ed. Claude Ménard and Mary M. Shirley (New York: Springer, 2005).

12. Congleton, *Perfecting Parliament: constitutional reform, liberalism, and the rise of Western democracy.*

13. Cavill, *The English parliaments of Henry VII, 1485-1504,* 46.

14. Congleton, *Perfecting parliament: constitutional reform, liberalism, and the rise of Western democracy.*

15. Christopher Hill, *The World Turned Upside Down; radical ideas during the English revolution* (London: Temple Smith, 1972).

16. Congleton, *Perfecting Parliament: constitutional reform, liberalism, and the rise of Western democracy.*

17. Daron Acemoglu and James A Robinson, 'Why did the west extend the franchise? inequality and growth in historical perspective,' (1997).

18. David F. Burg, *A World History of Tax Rebellions: an encyclopedia of tax rebels, revolts, and riots from antiquity to the present* (New York: Routledge, 2004).

19. Roger D Congleton, 'Economic development and democracy, does industrialization lead to universal suffrage?,' *Homo Economicus* 21, no. 2 (2004).

20. Congleton, *Perfecting Parliament: constitutional reform, liberalism, and the rise of Western democracy.*

21. Ronald Max Hartwell, 'Taxation in England during the industrial revolution,' *Cato Journal.* 1 (1981).

22. Laura E. Nym Mayhall, *The Militant Suffrage Movement: citizenship and resistance in Britain, 1860-1930* (New York: Oxford University Press, 2003).

23. Ibid.

24. Laurence Housman, 'No Truce to Tax-Resistance,' *Votes for Women*, 11 August 1911.
25. Charles Adams, *For Good and Wvil: the impact of taxes on the course of civilization* (London; New York: Madison Books, 1993).
26. 'Woman's Suffrage League Annual meeting,' *S. A. Register*, 17 May 1892.
27. John Hirst, 'Egalitarianism,' in *Sense & Nonsense in Australian Hstory*, ed. John Hirst (Melbourne: Black Inc. Agenda, 2006).

Chapter 3

1. Ilya Somin, *Democracy and Political Ignorance: why smaller government is smarter* (Stanford, California: Stanford Law Books, an imprint of Stanford University Press, 2013).
2. Ian McAllister, 'Civic education and political knowledge in Australia,' *Australian Journal of Political Science* 33, no. 1 (1998).
3. Bryan Douglas Caplan, *The Myth of the Rational Voter: why democracies choose bad policies* (Princeton: Princeton University Press, 2007).
4. Kaare Strøm, 'Delegation and accountability in parliamentary democracies,' *European Journal of Political Research* 37, no. 3 (2000).
5. John Ferejohn, 'Incumbent performance and electoral control,' *Public Choice* 50, no. 1 (1986).
6. Robin Hanson, *Overcoming Bias*, 14 March, 2009, http://www.overcomingbias.com/2009/03/yes-tax-ideas.html.
7. François Pétry and Benoît Collette, 'Measuring how political parties keep their promises: a positive perspective from political science,' *Do They Walk Like They Talk?* (Springer, 2009).
8. Edmund Burke, *The works of the Right Honourable Edmund Burke*, (Boston: Wells and Lilly, 1826), 2:95.

9. Casey B Mulligan and Charles G Hunter, 'The empirical frequency of a pivotal vote,' *Public Choice* 116, no. 1-2 (2003).
10. Caplan, *The Myth of the Rational Voter: why democracies choose bad policies.*
11. House of Commons Debates 11 November 1947 vol. 444 cc203-321, available at http://hansard.millbanksystems.com/commons/1947/nov/11/parliament-bill

Chapter 4

1. Rancière and Corcoran, *Hatred of Democracy.*
2. R. K. Sinclair, *Democracy and Participation in Athens* (Cambridge Cambridgeshire; New York: Cambridge University Press, 1988).
3. Peter P. Liddel, *Civic Obligation and Individual Liberty in Ancient Athens*, Oxford classical monographs (Oxford; New York: Oxford University Press, 2007).
4. James Wycliffe Headlam, *Election by Lot at Athens* (Cambridge University Press, 1891).
5. Cited in Jennifer Tolbert Roberts, *Athens on Trial: the antidemocratic tradition in Western thought* (Princeton, N.J.: Princeton University Press, 1994), 52.
6. Malcolm Crook, *Elections in the French Revolution: apprenticeship in democracy, 1789-1799* (Cambridge, UK; New York: Cambridge University Press, 1996).
7. Woodrow Wilson, 'The study of administration,' *Political Science Quarterly* 2, no. 2 (1887).
8. Dahl, *Democracy and its Critics*, 52.
9. Plato and G. M. A. Grube, *The Republic* (Indianapolis,: Hackett Pub. Co., 1974).
10. Karl R. Popper, *The Open Society and its Enemies* (London: Routledge, 1945).

11. David J. C. Shearman and Joseph Wayne Smith, *The Climate Change Challenge and the Failure of Democracy*. (Westport, Conn.: Praeger Publishers, 2007).

12. See, for instance Natalie Wolchover, *Life's Little Mysteries*, 28 February, 2012, http://www.livescience.com/18706-people-smart-democracy.html.

13. Sui Huang, 'When peers are not peers and don't know it: The Dunning-Kruger effect and self-fulfilling prophecy in peer-review,' *Bioessays* 35, no. 5 (2013).

14. Andrea E Waylen et al., 'Do expert drivers have a reduced illusion of superiority?,' *Transportation Research Part F: Traffic Psychology and Behaviour* 7, no. 4 (2004).

15. Scott Plous, *The Psychology of Judgment and Decision Making* (Philadelphia: Temple University Press, 1993).

16. Vicki Bier, 'Implications of the research on expert overconfidence and dependence,' *Reliability Engineering & System Safety* 85, no. 1 (2004).

17. Ibid.

18. Philip E. Tetlock, *Expert Political Judgment: How good is it? How can we know?* (Princeton, N.J.: Princeton University Press, 2005).

19. Bier, 'Implications of the research on expert overconfidence and dependence.'

20. Christina Romer and Jared Bernstein, *The Job Impact of the American Recovery and Reinvestment Act* (2009).

21. Rancière and Corcoran, *Hatred of Democracy*, 44.

22. Alan A. Lockhard, 'Sortition,' in *The Encyclopedia of Public Choice*, ed. Charles Kershaw Rowley and Friedrich Schneider (Dordrecht; Boston: Kluwer Academic Publishers, 2004), 532.

23. Headlam, *Election by Lot at Athens*.

Chapter 5

1. Mark Latham, *The Political Bubble: Why Australians Don't Trust Politics* (Pan Macmillan Australia, 2014).
2. John Hewson, 'The Politics of Tax Reform in Australia,' *Asia & the Pacific Policy Studies* (2014).
3. Nicholas Gruen, 'Making Fiscal Policy Flexibly Independent of Government,' *Agenda* 4, no. 3 (1997).
4. Stephen Bell, *Australia's Money Mandarins: the Reserve Bank and the politics of money* (Cambridge, England: Cambridge University Press, 2004).
5. Hewson, 'The Politics of Tax Reform in Australia.'
6. R. A. W. Rhodes, John Wanna, and Patrick Weller, 'Reinventing Westminster: how public executives reframe their world,' *The Policy Press* 36, no. 4 (2008).
7. Slavisa Tasic, 'Are Regulators Rational?,' *Journal des Economistes et des Etudes Humaines* 17, no. 1 (2011).
8. Chris Berg, *The Growth of Australia's Regulatory State: Ideology, Accountability and the Mega-Regulators* (Melbourne, Australia: Institute of Public Affairs, 2008).
9. Australian Securities and Investments Commission, *Inquiry into subsection 313(3) of the Telecommunications Act 1997: Submission by ASIC* (Parliament of Australia: Australian Securities and Investments Commission, 2014).
10. Bryan Firth, 'Judge says ASIC investigators failed to join the dots in their case against AWB,' *The Australian* 2009.
11. The story is told in Chris Berg, 'Accountability Goes Missing In Iraq Bank Note Scandal,' *The Drum*, 8 October 2013.
12. John B. Taylor, 'The Effectiveness of Central Bank Independence Versus Policy Rules', American Economic Association Annual Meeting (San Diego, California2013).

13. Roger Llewellyn Wettenhall, 'Quangos, Quagos and the Problems of Non-Ministerial Organization,' *Australian Journal of Public Administration* 42, no. 1 (1983).

Chapter 6

1. Patrick J Welch, 'Thomas Carlyle on utilitarianism,' *History of Political Economy* 38, no. 2 (2006).
2. J. P. Seigel, *Thomas Carlyle*, (London: Routledge & K. Paul, 1971).
3. Ibid.
4. Jonathan Rose, *The intellectual life of the British working classes* (New Haven, CT: Yale University Press, 2001), 42.
5. William Oliver Coleman, *Economics and its Enemies: two centuries of anti-economics* (Basingstoke, Hampshire; New York: Palgrave Macmillan, 2002).
6. Thomas Carlyle, 'Occasional Discourse on the Negro Question,' *Fraser's Magazine for Town and Country* 60 (1849).
7. Cited in Welch, 'Thomas Carlyle on utilitarianism.'
8. Carlyle, 'Occasional Discourse on the Negro Question.'
9. Ibid.
10. Cited in Gregory Claeys, *Encyclopedia of Nineteenth-Century Thought* (London; New York: Routledge, 2005).
11. John Stuart Mill, 'The Negro Question,' *Fraser's Magazine for Town and Country* 61 (1850).
12. Ibid.
13. Ludwig Von Mises, *Human Action: A Treatise on Economics* (Yale University, 1949).
14. Sandra Peart and David M. Levy, *The Street Porter and the Philosopher: conversations on analytical egalitarianism* (Ann Arbor: University of Michigan Press, 2008).
15. Maine, *Lectures on the early history of institutions.*

16. Lionel Robbins, 'Interpersonal comparisons of utility: a comment,' *The Economic Journal* (1938).

17. Thomas C Leonard, 'Retrospectives: Eugenics and economics in the progressive era,' *Journal of Economic Perspectives* (2005).

18. A. C. Pigou, *The Economics of Welfare*, 4th ed. (London: Macmillan and co., limited, 1932).

19. Arthur C Pigou, 'Social Improvement in the Light of Modern Biology,' *The Economic Journal* 17, no. 67 (1907).

20. Robert Cherry, 'Racial thought and the early economics profession,' *Review of Social Economy* 34, no. 2 (1976).

21. Ibid.

22. Leonard, 'Retrospectives: Eugenics and economics in the progressive era.'

23. Ibid.

24. Royal Meeker, 'Review of Cours d'économie politique,' *Political Science Quarterly* 25, no. 3 (1910).

25. Leonard, 'Retrospectives: Eugenics and economics in the progressive era.'

26. Sandra Peart and David M. Levy, *The 'vanity of the philosopher': from equality to hierarchy in postclassical economics* (Ann Arbor: University of Michigan Press, 2005), 81.

27. Coleman, *Economics and its Enemies: two centuries of anti-economics.*

28. William A. Niskanen, *Reflections of a Political Economist: selected articles on government policies and political processes* (Washington, D.C.: Cato Institute, 2008).

Chapter 7

1. Roberts, *Athens on Trial: the antidemocratic tradition in Western thought.*

2. Plato and G. M. A. Grube, *The Republic* (Indianapolis,: Hackett Pub. Co., 1974), 232.

3. Dominic Scott, 'Plato's critique of the democratic character,' *Phronesis* 45, no. 1 (2000).

4. Cited in Roger Swagler, 'Evolution and applications of the term consumerism: theme and variations,' *Journal of Consumer Affairs* 28, no. 2 (1994).

5. Cited in ibid.

6. John Paul II, 'Evangelium vitae, Encyclical letter on the value and inviolability of human life'.

7. Clive Hamilton and Richard Denniss, *Affluenza: when too much is never enough* (Crows Nest, NSW: Allen & Unwin, 2005).

8. Ian DeWeese-Boyd and Margaret DeWeese-Boyd, 'The Healthy City Versus the Luxurious City in Plato's Republic: Lessons About Consumption and Sustainability for a Globalizing Economy,' *Contemporary Justice Review* 10, no. 1 (2007).

9. Clive Hamilton, 'Marketing and Modern Consumerism', Third National Consumer Congress (Melbourne2006).

10. Jeffrey Sachs, *The Price of Civilization: reawakening American virtue and prosperity,* (New York: Random House, 2011).

11. Moses I Finley, 'Athenian demagogues,' *Past and Present* (1962).

12. Rancière and Corcoran, *Hatred of Democracy.*

13. Chris Berg, *In Defence of Freedom of Speech: From Ancient Greece to Andrew Bolt,* (Institute of Public Affairs; Mannkal Economic Education Foundation, 2012).

14. See, for instance, Chris Berg, 'Censorship standards come from a personal place,' *The Drum,* 26 February 2013.

15. Chris Berg, 'The true origins of anti-paternalism,' *The Drum,* 31 January 2012.

16. John Kleinig, *Paternalism* (Oxford: Clarendon Press, 1984).

17. Sarah Conly, *Against Autonomy: justifying coercive paternalism* (Cambridge: Cambridge University Press, 2013).

18. Ibid., 32.

19. Ibid., 24-25.
20. Robert A. Dahl, *On Political Equality* (New Haven: Yale University Press, 2006); Dahl, Democracy and its critics.
21. On this point, see Michael Huemer, *The Problem of Political Authority: an examination of the right to coerce and the duty to obey* (Houndmills, Basingstoke, Hampshire; New York: Palgrave Macmillan, 2013).
22. Conly, *Against Autonomy: justifying coercive paternalism*, 38.
23. Donald J Boudreaux and Eric Crampton, 'Truth and consequences: some economics of false consciousness,' *Independent Review* 8, no. 1 (2003).
24. Conly, *Against Autonomy: justifying coercive paternalism*, 17.
25. Niclas Berggren, 'Time for behavioral political economy? An analysis of articles in behavioral economics,' *The Review of Austrian Economics* 25, no. 3 (2012).
26. Jeremy Bentham, *Introduction to the Principles of Morals and Legislation* (Oxford: Clarendon Press, 1907).
27. Ministerial Council on Drug Strategy, National Alcohol Strategy 2006-2009 (Commonwealth of Australia, 2006).
28. Rebecca Johnson et al., 'Legal drug content in music video programs shown on Australian television on Saturday mornings,' *Alcohol and Alcoholism* 48, no. 1 (2013).
29. Heath Gilmore, 'Groping for truth in the fog of war,' *The Sydney Morning Herald*, 2 March 2014; Nick Collins, 'Winston Churchill's cigar airbrushed from picture,' *The Telegraph*, 15 June 2010.
30. Conly, *Against autonomy: justifying coercive paternalism*, 37-38.

Chapter 8

1. Richard J. Evans, *The Coming of the Third Reich* (London: A. Lane, 2003).
2. Ibid.
3. Roberts, *Athens on Trial: the antidemocratic tradition in Western thought.*
4. Aristotle and Stephen Everson, *The Politics*, (Cambridge England; New York: Cambridge University Press, 1988).
5. John Adams, *Works of John Adams, second President of the United States:. Vol. 6, Defence of the Constitutions Vol. III continued, Discourses on Davila, Letters* (S.l.: Little, Brown, 1856).
6. Ibid.
7. Alexander Hamilton, James Madison, and John Jay, *The Federalist papers* (Oxford; New York: Oxford University Press, 2008).
8. Adams, *Works of John Adams, second President of the United States:. Vol. 6, Defence of the Constitutions Vol. III continued.*
9. Dalibor Roháč, 'The unanimity rule and religious fractionalisation in the Polish-Lithuanian Republic,' *Constitutional Political Economy* 19, no. 2 (2008).
10. Adams, *Works of John Adams, second President of the United States:. Vol. 6, Defence of the Constitutions Vol. III continued*
11. Benjamin Constant, Etienne Hofmann, and Dennis O'Keeffe, *Principles of Politics Applicable to all Governments* (Indianapolis, Ind.: Liberty Fund, 2003).
12. Roháč, 'The unanimity rule and religious fractionalisation in the Polish-Lithuanian Republic.'
13. Ibid.
14. Alexander M. Bickel, *The Least Dangerous Branch: the Supreme Court at the bar of politics* (Indianapolis: Bobbs-Merrill, 1962).

15. Jeremy Waldron, 'The core of the case against judicial review,' *The Yale Law Journal* (2006).

16. Ilya Somin, 'Political ignorance and the countermajoritarian difficulty: A new perspective on the central obsession of constitutional theory,' *Iowa Law Review* 89 (2003).

17. Constant, Hofmann, and O'Keeffe, *Principles of Politics Applicable to all Governments.*

Chapter 9

1. George Grote, *Plato, and the other companions of Sokrates*, A new ed., 4 vols. (London,: J. Murray, 1888), 430.

2. Berg, *In Defence of Freedom of Speech: From Ancient Greece to Andrew Bolt.*

3. hris Berg, 'No wonder MPs are confused about security laws,' *The Drum*, 28 October 2014.

4. Downsize DC, 'The Read the Bills Act (RTBA),' https://downsizedc.org/etp/rtba/.

5. Thomas R Palfrey and Keith T Poole, 'The relationship between information, ideology, and voting behavior,' *American Journal of Political Science* (1987).

6. Victoria Shineman, 'Isolating the Effect of Compulsory Voting Laws on Political Sophistication: Exploiting Intra-national Variation in Mandatory Voting Laws between the Austrian Provinces,' (2012).

7. Malcolm Heath, 'Aristotle on natural slavery,' *Phronesis* (2008).

8. Anatole France, *The Red Lily* (New York,: Brentano's, 1898).

9. Thomas Piketty and Arthur Goldhammer, *Capital in the Twenty-First Century* (Cambridge Massachusetts: The Belknap Press of Harvard University Press, 2014).

10. Cited in Chris Berg, 'O'Farrell's campaign finance reforms are

abominable,' *The Drum*, 22 February 2012.

11. Gordon Tullock, 'The purchase of politicians,' *Western Economic Journal* 10, no. 3 (1972).

12. Stephen Ansolabehere, John M De Figueiredo, and James M Snyder, Why is there so little money in politics? (National bureau of economic research, 2003).

13. Friedrich A. von Hayek and Ronald Hamowy, *The Constitution of Liberty: the Definitive Edition*, (London; New York: Routledge, 2011).

14. Rancière and Corcoran, *Hatred of Democracy*, 48.

Conclusion

1. Friedrich A. von Hayek, *The Road to Serfdom*, Australian ed. (Sydney: Dymock's Book Arcade, 1944).

2. Phil Rosenzweig, 'Robert S. McNamara and the Evolution of Modern Management,' *Harvard Business Review*, no. December (2010).

3. David Halberstam, *The Best and the Brightest*, (New York,: Random House, 1972).

4. Nick Cater, *The Lucky Culture and the Rise of an Australian Ruling Class* (Sydney, N.S.W.: HarperCollinsPublishers, 2013).

5. Cited in Waldron, *God, Locke, and Equality: Christian foundations of John Locke's political thought*, 85-91.

Bibliography

Acemoglu, Daron, and James A Robinson. 'Why Did the West Extend the Franchise? Inequality and Growth in Historical Perspective.' (1997).

Adams, Charles. *For Good and Evil: The Impact of Taxes on the Course of Civilization*. London; New York: Madison Books, 1993.

Adams, John. *Works of John Adams, Second President of the United States:. Vol. 6, Defence of the Constitutions Vol. III Continued, Discourses on Davila, Letters*. S.l.: Little, Brown, 1856.

Ansolabehere, Stephen, John M De Figueiredo, and James M Snyder. 'Why Is There So Little Money in Politics?': National Bureau of Economic Research, 2003.

Aristotle, and Stephen Everson. *The Politics*. Cambridge Texts in the History of Political Thought. Cambridge England; New York: Cambridge University Press, 1988.

Australian Securities and Investments Commission. 'Inquiry into Subsection 313(3) of the Telecommunications Act 1997: Submission by ASIC.' Parliament of Australia: Australian Securities and Investments Commission, 2014.

Baker, Philip. *The Levellers: The Putney Debates*. London: Verso Books, 2007.

Bell, Stephen. *Australia's Money Mandarins: The Reserve Bank and the Politics of Money*. Cambridge., England: Cambridge University Press, 2004.

Benson, Bruce L. 'The Evolution of Law.' In *The Encyclopedia of Public Choice*, edited by Charles Kershaw Rowley and Friedrich Schneider, 2: 237-39. Dordrecht; Boston: Kluwer Academic Publishers, 2004.

Bentham, Jeremy. *Introduction to the Principles of Morals and Legislation*. Oxford: Clarendon Press, 1907.

Berg, Chris. 'Accountability Goes Missing in Iraq Bank Note Scandal.' *The Drum*, 8 October 2013.

Berg, Chris. 'Censorship Standards Come from a Personal Place.' *The Drum*, 26 February 2013.

Berg, Chris. *The Growth of Australia's Regulatory State: Ideology, Accountability and the Mega-Regulators*. Melbourne, Australia: Institute of Public Affairs, 2008.

Berg, Chris. *In Defence of Freedom of Speech: From Ancient Greece to Andrew Bolt*. Monographs on Western Civilisation. Institute of Public Affairs; Mannkal Economic Education Foundation, 2012.

Berg, Chris. 'Micro-Parties Tap into Dissatisfaction.' *The Drum*, 10 April 2014.

Berg, Chris. 'No Wonder Mps Are Confused About Security Laws.' *The Drum*, 28 October 2014.

Berg, Chris. 'O'Farrell's Campaign Finance Reforms Are Abominable.' *The Drum*, 22 February 2012.

Berg, Chris. 'The True Origins of Anti-Paternalism.' *The Drum*, 31 January 2012.

Berggren, Niclas. 'Time for Behavioral Political Economy? An Analysis of Articles in Behavioral Economics.' *The Review of Austrian Economics* 25, no. 3 (2012): 199-221.

Bickel, Alexander M. *The Least Dangerous Branch: The Supreme Court at the Bar of Politics*. Indianapolis: Bobbs-Merrill, 1962.

Bier, Vicki. 'Implications of the Research on Expert Overconfidence and Dependence.' *Reliability Engineering & System Safety* 85, no. 1 (2004): 321-29.

Boudreaux, Donald J, and Eric Crampton. 'Truth and Consequences: Some Economics of False Consciousness.' *Independent Review* 8, no. 1 (2003): 27-46.

Bryce, James Bryce. *Modern Democracies*. 2 vols London: Macmillan, 1921.

Buchanan, James M., and Gordon Tullock. *The Calculus of Consent: Logical Foundations of Constitutional Democracy*. The Collected Works of James M Buchanan. Indianapolis: Liberty Fund, 1999.

Bueno de Mesquita, Bruce, and Alastair Smith. *The Dictator's Handbook: Why Bad Behavior Is Almost Always Good Politics*. 1st ed. New York: PublicAffairs, 2011.

Burg, David F. *A World History of Tax Rebellions: An Encyclopedia of Tax Rebels, Revolts, and Riots from Antiquity to the Present*. New York: Routledge, 2004.

Burke, Edmund. T*he Works of the Right Honourable Edmund Burke*. Reprinted from the last London edition. ed. Boston,: Wells and Lilly, 1826.

Caplan, Bryan Douglas. *The Myth of the Rational Voter: Why Democracies Choose Bad Policies*. Princeton: Princeton University Press, 2007.

Carlyle, Thomas. 'Occasional Discourse on the Negro Question.' *Fraser's Magazine for Town and Country* 60 (February 1849).

Cater, Nick. *The lucky culture and the rise of an Australian ruling class.* Sydney, N.S.W.: HarperCollinsPublishers, 2013.

Cavill, P. R. *The English Parliaments of Henry VII, 1485-1504.* Oxford Historical Monographs. Oxford; New York: Oxford University Press, 2009.

Cherry, Robert. 'Racial Thought and the Early Economics Profession.' *Review of Social Economy* 34, no. 2 (1976): 147-62.

Claeys, Gregory. *Encyclopedia of Nineteenth-Century Thought.* London; New York: Routledge, 2005.

Coleman, William Oliver. *Economics and Its Enemies: Two Centuries of Anti-Economics.* Basingstoke, Hampshire; New York: Palgrave Macmillan, 2002.

Collins, Nick. 'Winston Churchill's Cigar Airbrushed from Picture.' *The Telegraph*, 2010, 15 June.

Congleton, Roger D. 'Economic Development and Democracy, Does Industrialization Lead to Universal Suffrage?'. *Homo Economicus* 21, no. 2 (2004): 283-311.

Congleton, Roger D. *Perfecting Parliament: Constitutional Reform, Liberalism, and the Rise of Western Democracy.* Cambridge; New York: Cambridge University Press, 2011.

Conly, Sarah. *Against Autonomy: Justifying Coercive Paternalism.* Cambridge: Cambridge University Press, 2013.

Constant, Benjamin, Etienne Hofmann, and Dennis O'Keeffe. *Principles of Politics Applicable to All Governments.* Indianapolis, Ind.: Liberty Fund, 2003.

Crook, Malcolm. *Elections in the French Revolution: Apprenticeship in Democracy, 1789-1799.* Cambridge, UK; New York: Cambridge University Press, 1996.

Dahl, Robert A. *Democracy and Its Critics.* New Haven: Yale University Press, 1989.

Dahl, Robert A. *On Political Equality.* New Haven: Yale University Press, 2006.

Day, David. *John Curtin: A Life.* Pymble, N.S.W.: HarperCollins, 1999.

DeWeese-Boyd, Ian, and Margaret DeWeese-Boyd. 'The Healthy City Versus the Luxurious City in Plato's Republic: Lessons About Consumption and Sustainability for a Globalizing Economy.' *Contemporary Justice Review* 10, no. 1 (2007): 115-30.

Dicey, Albert Venn. *The Privy Council: The Arnold Prize Essay, 1860.* London and New York,: Macmillan and co., 1887.

Dickenson, Jackie. "God Give Us Men': Attitudes Towards Parliamentary Representation in Australia 1929–33.' *History Australia* 8, no. 2 (2013).

Evans, Richard J. *The Coming of the Third Reich.* London: A. Lane, 2003.

Ferejohn, John. 'Incumbent Performance and Electoral Control.' *Public Choice* 50, no. 1 (1986): 5-25.

Finley, Moses I. 'Athenian Demagogues.' *Past and Present* (1962): 3-24.

Firth, Bryan. 'Judge Says ASIC Investigators Failed to Join the Dots in Their Case against AWB.' *The Australian*, 2009, 10 December

France, Anatole. *The Red Lily.* New York,: Brentano's, 1898.

Gilmore, Heath. 'Groping for Truth in the Fog of War.' *The Sydney Morning Herald*, 2014, 2 March.

Goot, Murray. 'Distrustful, Disenchanted and Disengaged? Polled

Opinion on Politics, Politicians and the Parties: An Historical Perspective.' Parliament and Public Opinion, Papers on Parliament 38 (2002): 27.

Greif, Avner. 'Commitment, Coercion and Markets: The Nature and Dynamics of Institutions Supporting Exchange.' In *Handbook of New Institutional Economics*, edited by Claude Ménard and Mary M. Shirley, 727-88. New York: Springer, 2005.

Griffith University, and Newspoll. 'Australian Constitutional Values Survey 2014.' 2014.

Grote, George. P*lato, and the Other Companions of Sokrates.* 4 vols London,: J. Murray, 1888.

Gruen, Nicholas. 'Making Fiscal Policy Flexibly Independent of Government.' *Agenda* 4, no. 3 (1997).

Halberstam, David. *The Best and the Brightest.* 1st ed. New York,: Random House, 1972.

Hamilton, Alexander, James Madison, and John Jay. *The Federalist Papers*. Oxford World's Classics. Oxford; New York: Oxford University Press, 2008.

Hamilton, Clive. 'Marketing and Modern Consumerism.' In Third National Consumer Congress. Melbourne, 2006.

Hamilton, Clive, and Richard Denniss. *Affluenza: When Too Much Is Never Enough*. Crows Nest, NSW: Allen & Unwin, 2005.

Hanson, Fergus. 'Lowy Institute Poll 2012.' Lowy Institute for International Policy, 2012.

Hanson, Robin. 'Yes, Tax Lax Ideas.' *Overcoming Bias*, 2009.

Hartwell, Ronald Max. 'Taxation in England During the Industrial Revolution.' *Cato Journal*, 1 (1981): 129.

Hayek, Friedrich A. von. *The Road to Serfdom*. Australian ed. Sydney: Dymock's Book Arcade, 1944.

Hayek, Friedrich A. von, and Ronald Hamowy. *The Constitution of Liberty: The Definitive Edition.* The Collected Works of F A Hayek. London; New York: Routledge, 2011.

Headlam, James Wycliffe. *Election by Lot at Athens.* Cambridge University Press, 1891.

Heath, Malcolm. 'Aristotle on Natural Slavery.' *Phronesis* (2008): 243-70.

Hewson, John. 'The Politics of Tax Reform in Australia.' *Asia & the Pacific Policy Studies* (2014).

Hill, Christopher. *The World Turned Upside Down; Radical Ideas During the English Revolution.* London,: Temple Smith, 1972.

Hill, Ronald J. 'The CPSU in a Soviet Election Campaign.' *Soviet Studies* 28, no. 4 (1976).

Hirst, John. 'Egalitarianism.' In *Sense & Nonsense in Australian History*, 149-73. Melbourne: Black Inc. Agenda, 2006.

Holt, J. C. 'The Prehistory of Parliament.' In *The English Parliament in the Middle Ages,* edited by R. G. Davies and Jeffrey Howard Denton, 1-28. Manchester: Manchester University Press, 1981.

Höpfl, Harro, and Martyn P. Thompson. 'The History of Contract as a Motif in Political Thought.' *The American Historical Review* 84, no. 4 (1979).

Hoppe, Hans-Hermann. 'Demokratie. Der Gott, Der Keiner Ist.' http://archive.lewrockwell.com/hoppe/hoppe9.html.

Housman, Laurence. 'No Truce to Tax-Resistance.' *Votes for Women,* 11 August 1911.

Huang, Sui. 'When Peers Are Not Peers and Don't Know It: The Dunning-Kruger Effect and Self-Fulfilling Prophecy in Peer-Review.' *Bioessays* 35, no. 5 (2013): 414-16.

Hudson, Phillip. 'Dysfunction Strips Faith in Politics.' *The Australian,* 10 October 2014.

Huemer, Michael. *The Problem of Political Authority: An*

Examination of the Right to Coerce and the Duty to Obey. Houndmills, Basingstoke, Hampshire; New York: Palgrave Macmillan, 2013.

Hume, David. 'Of the Original Contract.' In *Essays: Moral, Political and Literary*. Indianapolis: Liberty Fund, 1987.

John Paul II. *Evangelium Vitae*, Encyclical Letter on the Value and Inviolability of Human Life. http://www.vatican.va/holy_father/john_paul_ii/encyclicals/documents/hf_jp-ii_enc_25031995_evangelium-vitae_en.html.

Johnson, Rebecca, Emma Croager, Iain S Pratt, and Natalie Khoo. 'Legal Drug Content in Music Video Programs Shown on Australian Television on Saturday Mornings.' *Alcohol and Alcoholism* 48, no. 1 (2013): 119-25.

Karklins, Rasma. 'Soviet Elections Revisited: Voter Abstention in Noncompetitive Voting.' *The American Political Science Review* 80, no. 2 (1986).

Keane, John. *The Life and Death of Democracy*. 1st American ed. New York: W.W. Norton & Co., 2009.

Kleinig, John. *Paternalism*. Oxford: Clarendon Press, 1984.

Latham, Mark. *The Political Bubble: Why Australians Don't Trust Politics*. Pan Macmillan Australia, 2014.

Leonard, Thomas C. 'Retrospectives: Eugenics and Economics in the Progressive Era.' *Journal of Economic Perspectives* (2005): 207-24.

Liddel, Peter P. *Civic Obligation and Individual Liberty in Ancient Athens*. Oxford Classical Monographs. Oxford; New York: Oxford University Press, 2007.

Liebermann, F. *The National Assembly in the Anglo-Saxon Period*. Halle a. S.: M. Niemeyer, 1913.

Locke, John. *Two Treatises of Government*. Cambridge: Cambridge University Press, 1960.

Lockhard, Alan A. 'Sortition.' In *The Encyclopedia of Public Choice*, edited by Charles Kershaw Rowley and Friedrich Schneider, 2: 530-33. Dordrecht; Boston: Kluwer Academic Publishers, 2004.

Macpherson, C. B. *The Political Theory of Possessive Individualism: Hobbes to Locke*. Oxford: Oxford University Press, 2011.

Maine, Henry Sumner. *Lectures on the Early History of Institutions*. 7th ed. S.l.: J. Murray, 1914.

Mayhall, Laura E. Nym. *The Militant Suffrage Movement: Citizenship and Resistance in Britain, 1860-1930*. New York: Oxford University Press, 2003.

McAllister, Ian. 'Anu-Src Poll: Changing Views of Governance: Results from the Anupoll, 2008 and 2014.' ANU College of Arts and Social Sciences, 2014.

McAllister, Ian. 'Civic Education and Political Knowledge in Australia.' *Australian Journal of Political Science* 33, no. 1 (1998): 7-23.

McKechnie, William Sharp. *Magna Carta: A Commentary on the Great Charter of King John, with an Historical Introduction*. Glasgow: Maclehose, 1914.

Meeker, Royal. 'Review of Cours D'économie Politique.' *Political Science Quarterly* 25, no. 3 (1910): 543-45.

Mendle, Michael, ed. *The Putney Debates of 1647: The Army, the Levellers, and the English State*. Cambridge, U.K.; New York: Cambridge University Press, 2001.

Mill, John Stuart. 'The Negro Question.' *Fraser's Magazine for Town and Country* 61 (January 1850).

Mills, Charles W. *The Racial Contract*. Ithaca: Cornell University Press, 1997.

Ministerial Council on Drug Strategy. 'National Alcohol Strategy 2006-2009.' Commonwealth of Australia, 2006.

Mulligan, Casey B, and Charles G Hunter. 'The Empirical

Frequency of a Pivotal Vote.' *Public Choice* 116, no. 1-2 (2003): 31-54.

Niskanen, William *A. Reflections of a Political Economist: Selected Articles on Government Policies and Political Processes.* Washington, D.C.: Cato Institute, 2008.

O'Neill, Margot. 'Voters Should Have More Say in Policy.' In *Lateline.* Australian Broadcasting Corporation, 2014.

Oliver, Alex. 'Lowy Institute Poll 2014.' Lowy Institute for International Policy, 2014.

Palfrey, Thomas R, and Keith T Poole. 'The Relationship between Information, Ideology, and Voting Behavior.' *American Journal of Political Science* (1987): 511-30.

Pateman, Carole. *The Sexual Contract.* Cambridge: Polity, 1988.

Peart, Sandra, and David M. Levy. *The Street Porter and the Philosopher: Conversations on Analytical Egalitarianism.* Ann Arbor: University of Michigan Press, 2008.

Peart, Sandra, and David M. Levy. *The 'Vanity of the Philosopher': From Equality to Hierarchy in Postclassical Economics.* Ann Arbor: University of Michigan Press, 2005.

Pétry, François, and Benoît Collette. 'Measuring How Political Parties Keep Their Promises: A Positive Perspective from Political Science.' In *Do They Walk Like They Talk?*, 65-80: Springer, 2009.

Pigou, A. C. *The Economics of Welfare.* 4th ed. London: Macmillan and co., limited, 1932.

Pigou, Arthur C. 'Social Improvement in the Light of Modern Biology.' *The Economic Journal* 17, no. 67 (1907): 358-69.

Piketty, Thomas, and Arthur Goldhammer. *Capital in the Twenty-First Century.* Cambridge Massachusetts: The Belknap Press of Harvard University Press, 2014.

Plato, and G. M. A. Grube. *The Republic.* Indianapolis: Hackett Pub. Co., 1974.

Plous, Scott. *The Psychology of Judgment and Decision Making*. Philadelphia: Temple University Press, 1993.

Popper, Karl R. *The Open Society and Its Enemies*. London: Routledge, 1945.

Rancière, Jacques, and Steve Corcoran. *Hatred of Democracy* London New York: Verso, 2007.

Rhodes, R. A. W., John Wanna, and Patrick Weller. 'Reinventing Westminster: How Public Executives Reframe Their World.' *The Policy Press* 36, no. 4 (2008): 461-79.

Robbins, Lionel. 'Interpersonal Comparisons of Utility: A Comment.' *The Economic Journal* (1938): 635-41.

Roberts, Jennifer Tolbert. *Athens on Trial: The Antidemocratic Tradition in Western Thought*. Princeton, N.J.: Princeton University Press, 1994.

Roháč, Dalibor. 'The Unanimity Rule and Religious Fractionalisation in the Polish-Lithuanian Republic.' *Constitutional Political Economy* 19, no. 2 (2008): 111-28.

Romer, Christina, and Jared Bernstein. *The Job Impact of the American Recovery and Reinvestment Act*. 2009.

Rose, Jonathan. *The Intellectual Life of the British Working Classes*. New Haven, CT: Yale University Press, 2001.

Rosenzweig, Phil. 'Robert S. Mcnamara and the Evolution of Modern Management.' *Harvard Business Review*, December (2010).

Rundle, Guy. 'Greens a Major Party Now?' *Crikey*, 10 April 2014.

Sachs, Jeffrey. *The Price of Civilization: Reawakening American Virtue and Prosperity*. New York: Random House, 2011.

Scott, Dominic. 'Plato's Critique of the Democratic Character.' *Phronesis* 45, no. 1 (2000): 19-37.

Seigel, J. P. *Thomas Carlyle*. The Critical Heritage Series. London: Routledge & K. Paul, 1971.

Shearman, David J. C., and Joseph Wayne Smith. *The Climate Change Challenge and the Failure of Democracy*. Politics and the Environment,. Westport, Conn.: Praeger Publishers, 2007.

Shineman, Victoria. 'Isolating the Effect of Compulsory Voting Laws on Political Sophistication: Exploiting Intra-National Variation in Mandatory Voting Laws between the Austrian Provinces.' (2012).

Sinclair, R. K. *Democracy and Participation in Athens*. Cambridge Cambridgeshire; New York: Cambridge University Press, 1988.

Smith, Adam, and Ronald L. Meek. *Lectures on Jurisprudence*. Indianapolis: Liberty Classics, 1982.

Somin, Ilya. *Democracy and Political Ignorance: Why Smaller Government Is Smarter*. Stanford, California: Stanford Law Books, an imprint of Stanford University Press, 2013.

Somin, Ilya. 'Political Ignorance and the Countermajoritarian Difficulty: A New Perspective on the Central Obsession of Constitutional Theory.' *Iowa Law Review* 89 (2003): 1287.

Soutphommasane, Tim. 'When Wealth Becomes King, Democracy Is a Poor Subject.' *Sydney Morning Herald*, 18 June 2012.

Strøm, Kaare. 'Delegation and Accountability in Parliamentary Democracies.' *European Journal of Political Research* 37, no. 3 (2000): 261–89.

Swagler, Roger. 'Evolution and Applications of the Term Consumerism: Theme and Variations.' *Journal of Consumer Affairs* 28, no. 2 (1994): 347-60.

Swearer, Howard R. 'The Functions of Soviet Local Elections.' *Midwest Journal of Political Science* 5, no. 2 (1961).

Tacitus, Cornelius, and Anthony Richard Birley. *Agricola and Germany*. Oxford World's Classics. Oxford; New York: Oxford University Press, 1999.

Tasic, Slavisa. 'Are Regulators Rational?'. *Journal des Economistes et des Etudes Humaines* 17, no. 1 (2011).

Taylor, John B. 'The Effectiveness of Central Bank Independence Versus Policy Rules.' American Economic Association Annual Meeting. San Diego, California, 2013.

Tetlock, Philip E. *Expert Political Judgment: How Good Is It? How Can We Know?* Princeton, N.J.: Princeton University Press, 2005.

The University of Melbourne, Centre for Advancing Journalism, and Our Say. 'Citizens' Agenda: National Survey of Voters: Detailed Results.' 2013.

Tullock, Gordon. 'The Purchase of Politicians.' *Western Economic Journal* 10, no. 3 (1972): 354-55.

Von Mises, Ludwig. *Human Action: A Treatise on Economics.* Yale University, 1949.

Waldron, Jeremy. 'The Core of the Case against Judicial Review.' *The Yale Law Journal* (2006): 1346-406.

Waldron, Jeremy. *God, Locke, and Equality: Christian Foundations of John Locke's Political Thought.* Cambridge; New York: Cambridge University Press, 2002.

Walwyn, William. 'W Walwins Conceptions; for a Free Trade.' In *The Writings of William Walwyn*, edited by Jack R. McMichael and Barbara Taft. Athens and London: University of Georgia Press, 1989.

Waylen, Andrea E, Mark S Horswill, Jane L Alexander, and Frank P McKenna. 'Do Expert Drivers Have a Reduced Illusion of Superiority?'. *Transportation Research Part F: Traffic Psychology and Behaviour* 7, no. 4 (2004): 323-31.

Welch, Patrick J. 'Thomas Carlyle on Utilitarianism.' *History of Political Economy* 38, no. 2 (2006): 377-89.

Wettenhall, Roger Llewellyn. 'Quangos, Quagos and the Problems of Non-Ministerial Organization.' *Australian Journal of Public Administration* 42, no. 1 (1983): 5-52.

Wilson, Woodrow. 'The Study of Administration.' *Political Science Quarterly* 2, no. 2 (1887): 197-222.

Wolchover, Natalie. 'People Aren't Smart Enough for Democracy to Flourish, Scientists Say.' *Life's Little Mysteries*, 2012.

'Woman's Suffrage League Annual Meeting.' *S. A. Register*, 17 May 1892.

Woodhouse, A. S. P. *Puritanism and Liberty: Being the Army Debates (1647-9) from the Clarke Manuscripts with Supplementary Documents*. 2nd ed. London: Dent, 1974.

Wootton, David. 'The Levellers.' In *Democracy: The Unfinished Journey*, 508 Bc to Ad 1993, edited by John Dunn. Oxford; New York: Oxford University Press, 1992.

www.ingramcontent.com/pod-product-compliance
Lightning Source LLC
Chambersburg PA
CBHW050650270326
41927CB00012B/2960